Shelved

How to Get Your Self-Published Book Into Canadian Libraries, Register for PLR, and Start Earning Passive Income as an Author or Illustrator

Jacqueline Cooper & Lauren Hoste

Part of The Access Files

Published by **Little Goodbyes Press**

Copyright © 2025 Jacqueline Cooper

With research and editorial contributions by Lauren Hoste

Published by Little Goodbyes Press

All rights reserved.

No part of this publication may be reproduced, stored in a retrieval system, or transmitted in any form or by any means including electronic, mechanical, photocopying, recording, or otherwise without prior written permission from the publisher, except in the case of brief quotations used in reviews or scholarly articles.

Cooper, Jacqueline [and] Hoste, Lauren, author

Shelved: How to Get Your Self-Published Book Into Canadian Libraries, Register for PLR, and Start Earning Passive Income as an Author or Illustrator

Includes bibliographic references.

ISBN 978-1-0694647-3-6

1. Self-publishing in Canada, handbooks and manuals
2. Library acquisitions in Canada
3. Public Lending Right Program (Canada)
4. Authors and publishers in Canada
5. Book marketing in Canada
I. Title.

Cataloging provided by Publisher

This book is dedicated to the writers, illustrators, and creators who make space for their books on public shelves.

Thank you for sharing your work with us!

Contents

Why This Book Exists..1

Chapter 1: Why Libraries?..4
    Why Authors Pursue Libraries...4
    Not Just Public Libraries...6
    Little Free Libraries: A Quiet Visibility Tool.........................7
    Library and Archives Canada..9
    You Don't Need to Be Famous..10

Chapter 2: Understanding Canadian Libraries......................11
    How Canadian Libraries Are Structured............................11
    How Libraries Choose Which Books to Buy.....................12
    Where Canadian Libraries Actually Buy Books................14
    Yes, Libraries Do Want Self-Published Books...................16
    What Libraries Don't Want...16
    Should My Book Be Returnable?..17
    Do I Need a MARC Record?...18

Chapter 3: What is the PLR and Why You Want It.............20
    What Is the Public Lending Right Program?....................20
    How the Canadian PLR Program Works..........................21
    Who Benefits the Most from the PLR Program?..............26
    Real Earnings, Real People..27
    PLR Notice of File Closure..27
    Quick Links from This Chapter...28
    Deceased registrants (eligibility rules)................................28

Chapter 4: Getting into Library Vendor Systems (Before You Pitch)...29
    Step 1: Distribute Through IngramSpark or a Platform That Reaches Libraries..30
    Step 2: Set Canadian Metadata and Make It Returnable..........30

Step 3: How Ingram Sends Data to Library Vendors................31
Step 4: Check Before You Pitch..32
Sample Email to Vendors...33
What If Your Book Isn't Listed?..34
A Note About eBooks...34
Bottom Line..35

Chapter 5: How eBooks Reach Canadian Libraries (and What You Can Actually Control)..36
eBooks Aren't Ordered the Same Way as Print.......................36
Step 1: Use an Aggregator That Has Library Reach................37
Step 2: Libraries License, They Don't Buy..............................38
Step 3: Set Your Library Pricing Carefully..............................39
Step 4: Promote Your eBook's Library Availability.................40
Accessibility and EPUB Metadata..41
PLR and eBooks: Yes, They Count..41

Chapter 6: What About Audiobooks?..................................43
How Libraries Get Audiobooks..43
How to Make Your Audiobook Available to Libraries............44
Pricing and Discovery..45
Audiobooks and PLR..45

Chapter 7: Getting Your Book Ready for Libraries............47
ISBNs: The First Step to Being Discoverable..........................47
Preserving Your Book in the National Collection...................48
Making Your Book Lendable Through LAC............................48
CIP: Not Available for Self-Published Books..........................49
Trim Size and Format...50
Thinking About Accessibility...51
Helpful Tools for Accessible Self-Publishing..........................53
Metadata, BISAC and THEMA Codes.....................................55
More About BISAC Codes...59
More about THEMA Codes..60
Writing a Library-Ready Description......................................61

What Is ONIX Metadata? (And Why You Probably Don't Need It)..62
Metadata Mistakes to Avoid..63

Chapter 8: The Truth About Platform-Issued ISBNs..........67
Most Publishing Advice Isn't Written for Canadians...............67
Who Is the Publisher?..67
Legal Deposit Isn't Guaranteed..68
PLR Eligibility Depends on Discoverability............................69
Libraries Don't Order from Amazon or Indigo......................69
You Can Still Fix It..70
The Smart Choice for Canadian Authors..................................71

Chapter 9: PLR-Eligible Content vs. Library-Friendly..........72
What Makes a Book Eligible for PLR?......................................73
Books That *Don't* Qualify for PLR but the Library Might Want Them..73
What Makes a Book Library-Friendly?......................................77
Why Some Books Qualify for PLR but Never Earn a Dime....77
What About Donating Your Book?..78
Where These Paths Overlap..79
If You're Focused on Library Shelving but Not PLR...............80

Chapter 10: Who Qualifies for the PLR Program..................82
Authors and Editors..83
What About Illustrators?..84
Other Contributors Who May Qualify......................................85

Chapter 11: Building Your Outreach Toolkit........................88
Why a Spreadsheet Matters (Even a Simple One)....................89
How to Build Your Own Contact List......................................89
Submitting via Forms: What to Expect......................................91
A Note on Outcomes (and Uncertainty)....................................92
When Direct Emails Work Better..93
How Many Follow-Ups Is Too Many?..94

Chapter 12: Writing Your Pitch..96
    Be Clear, Not Clingy...96
    What Libraries Actually Want to Know.............................97
    What Not to Say in your Pitch..100
    Should You Offer a Free Copy to the Library?...............101
    Tone and Timing...102
    Following Up...102

Chapter 13: If You're Credited, You Count: Tips for Non-Author Creators.. 104
    Libraries Care About the Book, Not Who Sends It.......105
    You Can Be the One to Reach Out to Libraries..............106
    Why It's Worth Doing..108
    How PLR Applies to You...109
    Take the Initiative...110

Chapter 14: Timing Your Pitch and When to Follow-Up..111
    Understanding Library Timing Cycles.............................111
    Summer...112
    Late Summer/Early Fall..112
    Late Fall..113
    How Long to Wait Before Following Up.........................113
    Sample Follow-Up Email (After No Response)..............115
    Sample Follow-Up Email (After Submitting Through a Form) 116
    Keeping Track Without Losing Steam.............................117

Chapter 15: How and When to Apply for the PLR Program in Canada...119
    Who Can Apply?...119
    When to Apply..120
    Where to Register for the PLR Program..........................121
    Step-by-Step Walkthrough...122
    Common Mistakes to Avoid with the PLR Program.....123

    Are PLR Payments Taxable?..125
    Does PLR Count Against Grant Limits?..................................125
    Other Programs: Provincial Equivalents and Alternatives.....126
    Don't Forget to Reapply for the PLR Each Calendar Year....126

Chapter 16: Leveraging Your Library Success......................128
    Tracking Your Book's Presence in Libraries.............................128

Chapter 17: Other Programs That Support Canadian Creators...134
    Beyond the PLR: What Else Is Out There?..............................134
    Provincial Grant Programs for Authors and Illustrators........134
    Access Copyright – Payback Program..140
    Tracking Your Eligibility and Deadlines...................................141
    Using Your Library Footprint to Support Grants...................142

What Happens Next..144

Appendix A: Key Library & PLR Sites...................................146
    Library and Archives Canada (LAC)..146
    Public Lending Right (PLR) Program......................................147

Appendix B: Provincial Opportunities for Creators...........148

Appendix C: PLR Program Rules Summary.......................151

Appendix D: From PCIP to MARC – Example Template 153
    Creating a MARC Record?..155

Appendix E: Library-Ready Checklist....................................156
    Quick Checklist: Is Your Book Ready for Library Outreach?
   156
    Book Format & Metadata..156
    Distribution & Listings...157
    Outreach-Ready Materials...157

Glossary..159

About the Authors...163

Why This Book Exists

I didn't set out to become a marketer. When I started creating my first book, *Bye-Bye, Boobies*, I just wanted it to find its way into the hands of families who needed it. For me, that meant making sure it could be found in public libraries.

But I quickly ran into a wall. Like many indie authors, I had presumed I could simply donate a copy of my book to my local branch and that would be enough. It turns out, that's rarely how it works. These days, due to the volume of books that are being produced every year, most libraries don't add randomly donated books to their shelves. Even more surprising was that if you do send a book to the library as a donation, it likely will be routed straight to fundraising sales without a librarian ever seeing it.

So I started researching how books *actually* make it into libraries, not just in my area, but across Canada and beyond and what I found surprised me. Most of the guidance available was aimed at U.S. authors, which was a good starting point, because the basic principles were there. How libraries select and purchase books including using trusted vendors, evaluating metadata, and prioritizing community interest are pretty universal.

As I continued to look into Canadian libraries, I stumbled across the Public Lending Right (PLR) program, which is a Canadian fund that pays creators when their books are held in library collections. I'd never heard of it before, and most self-published authors I knew hadn't either. It's one of the few programs that rewards authors not for sales, but for accessibility something libraries are all about.

That's when I realized all of this information needed to be easier to find. If you're a self-published author or illustrator whether you're in Canada or elsewhere, understanding how libraries make decisions can help your book reach more readers, in more meaningful ways, over time.

This book will help you:

- Understand what PLR is (and who qualifies)

- Get your book into libraries (not just donate and hope)

- Avoid common metadata and pitching mistakes

- Treat libraries as a meaningful part of your book's life, not just an afterthought

While this book was written from a Canadian perspective, the strategies inside can be applied across borders.. Because I believe whether you live in a small town or a big city, your book deserves a place on public shelves and this is your starting point.

A note of thanks here to my co-author, Lauren, who helped carry this book across the finish line. Researching the inner workings of library systems, vendor pipelines, and government programs took more digging than I expected, and I'm grateful for the steady hand (and steady Googling) that helped shape this into a clear, usable guide.

For clickable links, updates, and bonus resources related to this book, visit:

www.littlegoodbyes.ca/books/shelved

Let's begin.

Chapter 1: Why Libraries?

You've probably already imagined seeing your book in a reader's hands but have you pictured it on a public library shelf?

For many authors, getting a book into a public library feels like validation. It means someone beyond your immediate circle believed your work belonged on a shelf, where anyone could discover it. It's not about bestseller lists or viral sales, it's about *readership,* about *access.* It's about knowing that your story, your voice, your effort will be available to someone who needs it, even if they can't afford to buy it. Let's face it, books can be very expensive, especially for self-published authors.

Plus libraries serve communities in ways bookstores can't. They lend, recommend, archive, and preserve. And when your book becomes part of that system, it becomes part of a cultural record that lives beyond the ebb and flow of online sales.

Why Authors Pursue Libraries

Authors, especially indie authors, often underestimate just how valuable library inclusion can be. It's not just a personal milestone (although it is that). It's also strategic, and a passive form of marketing as you'll see.

Visibility and Discovery

Libraries put your book in front of readers who would never stumble across it online, especially when they place it in their new books section, local author section, or even their Canadian content section. That kind of visibility builds trust, credibility, and discoverability, all without spending a dime on ads or chasing social media algorithms.

Trust and Credibility

A book on a library shelf feels official, vetted. Many readers discover authors in libraries and go on to buy other books later, or even the same one that they read to add to their personal home library collection, or to give as a gift.

Educational Reach

If your book is relevant to students, parents, educators, or researchers, library systems amplify its reach.

Passive Income (in some countries)

In places like Canada, the UK, and Australia, authors can receive annual payments when their books are held in public libraries. More on this, later in the book.

Some authors seek out libraries because they want to support equitable access. Some do it for the quiet thrill of being catalogued. Some do it for the long game, keeping a title circulating for years after its sales peak. And some do it because they're building a career and want to show up in all the places books live.

Not Just Public Libraries

When we talk about "libraries," we're not only talking about the local branch down the street (though that's a great place to start). Authors and illustrators also submit their books to:

- National libraries, like Library and Archives Canada or the British Library, which collect every book published in their country.
- School libraries, where your book may be read aloud or included in classroom libraries.

- Hospital and clinic collections *(often stocked with books on parenting, grief, or recovery)*
- Rehabilitation and wellness centres
- Prison libraries *(which may accept donations, especially for literacy and self-help)*
- University or college collections *(for books with academic or creative merit)*
- Specialty libraries *(e.g., Indigenous cultural centres, multilingual collections, or community-specific spaces)*
- Book Clubs

Some of these venues may not have purchasing budgets, but they often welcome donated or discounted copies, especially if your book aligns with their audience or mission.

Little Free Libraries: A Quiet Visibility Tool

You might also consider donating a few copies to Little Free Libraries in your area. These small, community-run book boxes won't count toward PLR earnings or official library circulation but they can quietly introduce your work to local readers in a meaningful way.

Shelved

For authors of children's books, poetry, memoirs, or niche nonfiction, this kind of placement offers gentle, long-term visibility. A parent might discover your book during a park visit. A teacher might pick it up and recommend it to their school librarian. A reader who enjoys it may look for your name again.

If you have extra copies on hand, especially slightly imperfect proofs or overstock, it can be a thoughtful, low-cost way to let your book find its people.

Of course, not everyone can afford to donate copies, and there's no pressure to do so. But for those who can, it's one more way to build quiet momentum without cold emails or paid ads.

Optional Label Text (Inside Front Cover or Title Page)

This book was donated by the author to share freely.

If you enjoy it, please pass it on or ask your local library to carry it.

You could print this on a sticker, handwrite it, or include it as a stamp or insert just enough to signal authorship and invite the next step.

To find local registered Little Free Libraries near you, visit their site at www.littlefreelibrary.org/map

Library and Archives Canada

In Canada, Library and Archives Canada requires publishers and self-published authors to deposit copies of all works that have been assigned ISBNs by them. This isn't a sales pitch, it's a legal deposit and a powerful milestone. It means your work becomes part of the permanent national collection. It means it exists.

Other countries around the world have similar systems, and this kind of deposit is often the first step toward being taken seriously as a published author.

In addition, submitting your book to LAC also makes it discoverable in Voilà, Canada's national union catalogue, which is connected to the global WorldCat system. Of course, it doesn't guarantee library sales, but it gives your book a permanent, searchable presence, not just in Canada; which makes it an invaluable step toward being found, borrowed, and catalogued by libraries across Canada and beyond.

You Don't Need to Be Famous

One of the best things about libraries is that they aren't chasing trends or hype. They're curated by people who care about books and the communities they work in. They buy books they believe their patrons will use, love, or need.

You don't have to be a household name to get into libraries. But you *do* have to understand what they're looking for and that's what the rest of this book is here to help you with.

Chapter 2: Understanding Canadian Libraries

If you're an author, illustrator other creator trying to get your book into public libraries, it helps to understand how those libraries actually work and how they choose what goes on the shelves. This chapter explains who runs the show, how decisions are made, and why your self-published title can absolutely belong there.

How Canadian Libraries Are Structured

Canada doesn't have one single library system. Instead, it's layered across federal, provincial, and municipal levels.

Federal

The federal government supports national programs (like Library and Archives Canada and the Public Lending Right program), but it doesn't buy books for public libraries.

Provincial/Territorial

Each province has a library services branch that coordinates shared systems, training, and interlibrary loan services.

Municipal

Local libraries, the ones that are run by your town, city, or sometimes municipality, are the ones that actually *buy books*. Most decisions about acquisitions, programming, and shelving happen here.

Some rural areas use regional systems that serve multiple towns, and Indigenous libraries may operate independently with unique funding and community-driven collections.

The bottom line, you're pitching your book to local gatekeepers not a national buyer.

How Libraries Choose Which Books to Buy

I'm sure it's no surprise to learn that librarians don't browse Indigo or Amazon looking for titles to stock in their library. Instead, they follow acquisition policies and buy almost exclusively through trusted library vendors.

These trusted vendors often will offer things like:

- Discounted pricing
- Consolidated invoicing
- Pre-applied barcodes and spine labels
- MARC records for cataloguing
- Returnable options and Canadian distribution

Librarians also consult and/or consider:

- Patron or staff requests
- Awards and reviews
- Community needs (especially local authors)

What I discovered is that libraries rarely accept books that arrive unsolicited and even when they do, there's no guarantee those books will be added to the collection. Many are quietly routed to used book sales or fundraising bins.

Where Canadian Libraries Actually Buy Books

If you want a Canadian library to buy your book, you need to make it easy for them. Here are the most common vendors used by Canadian libraries.

Whitehots

One of the largest suppliers and used by many public libraries across Canada.

https://www.whitehots.com/

TinLids

Specializes in children's books and also serves school libraries.

https://tinlids.ca/

United Library Services (ULS)

Smaller-scale but still used by many librarians.

https://www.uls.com/

BC Libraries Cooperative

Some consider this to be a bit more Western Canada focused, including support for Indigenous libraries.

https://bc.libraries.coop/

Ingram / Baker & Taylor

Without a doubt B&T is the one that came up the most for me when I started my research. While they are the preferred source for acquiring books for libraries in the U.S., Canadian libraries can order from them but not as frequently as the ones listed above.

https://www.baker-taylor.com/

What I also found was that many public libraries *must* order through a preferred vendor due to public sector purchasing policies, budget policies, cataloguing workflow, or bulk order systems. That means even if they *want* your book, they can't always buy it unless it's listed where they shop.

One thing to remember, as a self-published author, if you distribute your book through IngramSpark with Canadian metadata and returnable terms, it can show up in these vendors' portals, but not always automatically.

We'll walk through that process of checking to ensure it is with those vendors before you pitch to the libraries later in the book.

Yes, Libraries Do Want Self-Published Books

In talking to many authors, I discovered that there's a persistent myth that libraries won't stock indie or self-published titles. But in reality, libraries are *actively trying* to represent more local voices, underrepresented authors, and diverse content.

What Libraries Don't Want

What they don't want is extra work. A self-published book that's hard to order, hard to catalogue, or comes with strings attached *(like only being available via the author's website)* is more likely to be skipped.

To be library-ready, your book should be:

- Professionally printed (no coil bindings or homemade covers)
- Available through standard vendors (see above)
- Catalogued with an ISBN
- Ideally returnable (see below)
- Requested by patrons or community members
- Relevant to local readers (Canadian content matters)

Shelved

Many library systems in Canada also have "local author" sections, indie showcases, or small press collections that welcome self-published books. Your job is to position your book in a way that works within their system, not outside of it.

Should My Book Be Returnable?

Most libraries prefer to buy books that are listed as returnable through their vendors *(like IngramSpark or Whitehots)*. This isn't because they plan to send it back, it's a safety net for them in case:

- The book arrives damaged or misprinted
- The wrong edition *(e.g. hardcover vs. softcover)* is sent
- The title was approved, but a budget change or processing issue occurs right away

Once a book is catalogued, most libraries will keep it in their collection *for at least two years*, and often much longer. This is important not just for passive marketing and expanded access to your book, but, if you are eligible, for PLR payments. Remember PLR payments can last up to 25 years for one title.

So "returnable" is about protecting the purchase process, not second-guessing your book's value.

Tip: IngramSpark lets you choose "returnable" and "deliverable" in Canada. Some libraries will avoid non-returnable listings altogether when they are deciding to purchase a book for their collection.

Do I Need a MARC Record?

Not always, but a lot of the time, having one can help you get through the door.

What is a MARC Record?

A MARC record is a digital cataloguing file that librarians can import directly into their systems. It contains your ISBN, author name, title, subject headings, and other key metadata.

In Canada:

- If your book is in a vendor catalogue, like Whitehots or B&T, those suppliers often generate MARC records for libraries that purchase through them.

- If you're only on Amazon or IngramSpark, and you're pitching libraries directly, it's a good idea to provide a MARC record yourself, or at least be able to offer one.

Tip: If you've already created a PCIP block for your copyright page, that info can be used to generate a MARC record later. See the sample MARC record based in Appendix D.

Chapter 3: What is the PLR and Why You Want It

If you're a Canadian author, illustrator or other creator and your work is in a public library, you could be getting paid for it. Not through sales or royalties, but through something called the Public Lending Right Program (PLR). This is a little-known, but incredibly valuable source of passive income that rewards authors when their books are available in libraries across Canada.

Of course, PLR programs exist in many other countries, including the UK, Australia, and several EU nations but this book focuses solely on the Canadian system administered by the Canada Council for the Arts.

What Is the Public Lending Right Program?

The PLR is a federal program administered by the Canada Council for the Arts. It pays creators whose books are held in public libraries. The idea is simple: If your book is available for free borrowing, you're still contributing intellectual labour, and this program recognizes that.

Each year, the program surveys a sample of public libraries across the country. If your book is found in their holdings, you get a payment. The more libraries that carry your book, the higher your payout, up to a yearly maximum (in 2025 that was $4,500).

How the Canadian PLR Program Works

Each title only needs to be registered once.

However, and this is important to note, you must register it *within five years of its original publication date.* After that window, even if your book is in libraries, you can't add it to the program.

The great news is once a book is accepted into the program, it can remain in the PLR system for up to 25 years, paying annually, provided:

- It continues to be held in libraries
- You confirm your file during the annual update period
- Your contact and banking information stays current

Remember, if you skip the yearly update, your payments will be paused even if your book is still being found, so be sure to add it to your calendar to update this each year!

There is also a minimum annual payment threshold of $50. If your total calculated payment across all registered titles is less than $50 in a given year, no payment is issued. Once your total passes that threshold, you'll receive the full amount.

Important to Note: You may see outdated advice saying your book needs to be priced at $50 or more to qualify for payment this is not true. The PLR program does not require a minimum retail price, and you do not need to declare pricing during registration. Your payment is based solely on how many sampled libraries hold your book and whether your total calculated payout reaches $50 or more across all titles for that year.

How Many Books Can You Register?

Each year, you can register up to 20 new titles, across all roles (author, illustrator, translator, etc.). Currently, that's a hard annual cap even if you've published more.

Over time, as you continue to create works, you can accumulate quite a large catalogue inside the program. But each year, the PLR system will only pay for up to 25 titles per contributor role. That means 25 as author, 25 as illustrator, and so on.

One thing that is important to remember, you don't choose which 25 books get counted; the system automatically selects the most widely held titles in the national library sample. So even if you've registered 40 books as an author or illustrator, only the 25 most commonly found in libraries will count toward your payment in any given year.

Payouts

Your annual PLR payment is based on:

- How many of the sampled libraries hold your book
- Your contribution type (sole author, co-author, illustrator, etc.)
- The book format (print, audio, digital)
- Annual program funding and how many creators are in the pool

Payments vary each year, but every February you'll receive a statement showing your books that have been included in their survey, followed by a direct deposit to your bank account.

PLR Hit Rate

Each year, the Canada Council sets the PLR "hit rate," which is the *amount paid per copy of a book found in the sampled libraries*. This rate varies depending on how long a book has been registered and the total funding available in that year.

PLR Payment Calculation Example

An illustrator has contributed to a children's book, which was registered 7 years ago and found in 5 libraries.

The hit rate in 2024–25 was $61.47. The title was found 5 times. The illustrator's percentage share is 50%. Their time adjustment is 80%.

The hit rate ($61.47) is multiplied by the number of times the title was found (5) x the percentage share (0.50) x the time adjustment (0.8). The payment amount for this title is $122.94.

If the illustrator has other titles registered with the program, those payments will be calculated and then aggregated in the payment sent to the illustrator.

As this rate varies every year, I felt it was important to include this example as well as the link current and past rates on the official funding breakdown page to avoid any confusion and to ensure you can check in the future for any changes:

https://publiclendingright.ca/payments

Who Benefits the Most from the PLR Program?

As the example for the payment calculation shows, the PLR isn't just for bestselling authors, although I'm sure they are enrolled. In fact, self-published writers, illustrators, children's authors, translators, poets often benefit the most from this program as they don't all have best selling books and why I think it is worth an extra bit of effort to get their books into libraries.

PLR is one of the rare systems where a single copy of your book in a few libraries can still earn you money. Multiply that across dozens of libraries, and the passive income adds up fairly quickly.

And for children's authors in particular, PLR can become a powerful income stream. Why? Because libraries often buy more copies of picture books, hold them for longer, and share them between branches, all of which increases your odds of getting paid.

Real Earnings, Real People

It's not uncommon for authors with just one or two books to receive $300–$1,200 per year, depending on library presence. And those contributors with larger catalogs, especially in high-circulation genres like fiction, kids' lit or even poetry, may receive several thousand dollars annually.

Now for the best part, once your books are in the system, that income is passive. No marketing, no new release, just reliable payment year after year, as long as you confirm your contact and banking information is current annually and your books stay on shelves.

PLR Notice of File Closure

Individual titles are automatically retired after 25 years, or after 5 consecutive years of not being found in the annual library sample. However, if you have other titles listed, your account will continue to be active.

Once all of your registered titles have been retired from the program, your PLR file will be closed. At that point, you'll receive a formal notice confirming that your file has been fully closed and you are no longer an active registrant.

Your file is also closed if you are deceased.

Quick Links from This Chapter

Register a new title for the PLR:

https://publiclendingright.ca/update-your-file/register-new-title

Annual file update:

https://publiclendingright.ca/update-your-file/update-contact-info

Deceased registrants (eligibility rules)

At this time the PLR does not pay the estates of people who are deceased. It is important that your will notes your participation in this program and/or that your estate planner is aware that you are registered for this program so that they can close your account.

Chapter 4: Getting into Library Vendor Systems (Before You Pitch)

When I first started researching how to get my book into libraries, as I mentioned earlier, most of the advice I found was written for U.S. authors. It didn't reflect how Canadian libraries work or how they order books and other materials, and even for the U.S. system, almost none of it mentioned the importance of vendor systems.

So let's get one thing clear early, libraries don't buy books directly from Indigo or Amazon. They buy through vendors that are approved for purchases, and if your book isn't listed with those vendors, they won't be able to order it, no matter how much they like it.

Of course, some librarians will accept donations directly from you, so feel free to skip this if chapter that's the case.

This chapter walks you through how self-published books get from IngramSpark (or another platform) into vendors like Whitehots and B&T and how to check if you're actually visible before you start your outreach.

Step 1: Distribute Through IngramSpark or a Platform That Reaches Libraries

In this chapter I reference IngramSpark because it's probably the most common route Canadian self-published authors use to make their print books widely available that as many preferred vendors as selections. But the same general principles apply to other platforms that distribute through Ingram's catalog like Draft2Digital (D2D) or publishing aggregators.

The key point is this, you need a distributor that pushes your book into the same databases that Canadian library vendors use. The great thing I've learned is that Ingram does this automatically once your book is published but only if your settings are correct, so be sure to check your metadata if you find that your book is not being listed by the vendors.

Step 2: Set Canadian Metadata and Make It Returnable

Here's what you need to check in your IngramSpark (or aggregator) setup:

- Country of publication: Set to Canada
- Language: English or French (depending on your book)

- Returnability: Set your book to returnable

- Set a wholesale discount: Typically 40–55%

One thing that is consistent for both U.S. libraries as well as Canadian ones, is that books that are marked as "non-returnable" or have ultra-low discounts are often excluded from vendor catalogs. Even if your book makes it into the system, a library may skip over it if it's not returnable or priced too high, especially if they've been burned by self-published titles in the past.

Step 3: How Ingram Sends Data to Library Vendors

Once your book is published through Ingram, it's added to their global catalog, which feeds into a long list of retailers and vendors including:

- Whitehots
- Brodart
- Baker & Taylor (B&T)
- Bound2Learn
- EBSCO

But it's important to remember that just because Ingram sends them the data, it doesn't mean your book appears in every vendor's system.

Some vendors manually review titles before they go live in their own systems. Others won't bother listing your book unless a librarian specifically requests it (or the author/illustrator). Since there's no public checklist or timeline for this, it's worth checking to make sure your title is in there before you start filling in the forms and sending the emails to libraries asking them to include your book in their collection.

Step 4: Check Before You Pitch

After speaking with a few authors that had tried and failed to get their books into libraries, but really were not sure why, I can say that you don't want to email 20 libraries only to have them respond with, *"We can't find this in our system."* It's frustrating for everyone and it makes you look unprepared. So before you start contacting libraries, send a quick email to the major vendors listed here asking if your ISBN is active in their system.

You're not asking them to feature your book or order a copy. You're just checking to make sure it's visible and available to library buyers.

Sample Email to Vendors

Here's a simple template you can use when reaching out:

Subject: ISBN Availability Inquiry

Hi [Vendor name],

I've recently published a book through IngramSpark with the following ISBN: [insert ISBN].

Could you please confirm whether it is currently listed in your system and available to libraries for order?

Thank you for your time,

[Your Name]

You can adapt this slightly depending on whether you're emailing Whitehots, B&T, or someone else. You should be able to find contact emails available on their websites under support or acquisition departments.

What If Your Book Isn't Listed?

If a vendor replies that your book isn't in their system:

- Double-check your Ingram metadata and settings
- Make sure your book is returnable and has a standard wholesale discount
- Confirm that you've opted in to "Global Distribution" (or the equivalent setting on your aggregator)
- Wait a week or two and check back again, sometimes books take time to populate

If nothing changes, you can follow up again or look into direct vendor submission, which is sometimes possible with local or niche-interest titles.

A Note About eBooks

This chapter focuses on print books, which are the primary format Canadian public libraries order through vendors like Whitehots and B&T.

If you're distributing eBooks, library access is a whole different story typically involving OverDrive, Hoopla, Bibliotheca, or direct digital lending platforms. That's beyond the scope of this chapter, but it's worth knowing that eBook and print vendor systems are often completely separate.

Bottom Line

If your goal is to get into Canadian libraries, visibility matters. IngramSpark and other distributors can get your book into the pipeline but it's up to you to make sure the listing is actually live and orderable.

A quick check with vendors before you pitch libraries can save you time, avoid confusion, and help you come across as a professional, not just another hopeful author with a book to sell.

Chapter 5: How eBooks Reach Canadian Libraries (and What You Can Actually Control)

Getting your eBook into Canadian libraries is a completely different process than getting a print copy on the shelf. Different platforms, different vendors, and different rules. It comes as no surprise, most of the "get your eBooks into libraries!" advice online is either U.S.-focused or skips the fine print.

This chapter walks you through what *actually* happens when you try to make your eBook available to libraries in Canada and what you can (and can't) control as a self-published author.

eBooks Aren't Ordered the Same Way as Print

Public libraries in Canada usually order print books through vendors like Whitehots or B&T, but they don't use those same vendors for eBooks.

Instead, they license digital books through digital lending platforms. The big ones in Canada are:

- OverDrive / Libby (most common)
- Hoopla
- Bibliotheca
- BiblioBoard (used less often, but still around)
- Cantook (especially in Quebec and French-language collections)

You can't just upload your eBook to IngramSpark and expect it to show up in Libby. Even if you check the "library distribution" box, it won't automatically get picked up by public library systems. So what can you do to get your books ready to be ordered by the library?

Step 1: Use an Aggregator That Has Library Reach

To get your eBook into Canadian libraries, you'll usually need to use a distributor or aggregator with direct relationships to these platforms. Common options include:

- **Draft2Digital (D2D):** lets you opt into library distribution through OverDrive, Hoopla, and others
- **Kobo Writing Life:** distributes to libraries via OverDrive if your eBook is published through them

- **Cantook:** distributes to libraries both eBooks and audio books
- **StreetLib:** has limited reach into Bibliotheca and other platforms
- **PublishDrive:** offers some global library distribution

Each aggregator takes a cut of your royalties, and each has different terms, but they handle the technical upload and make your eBook visible to library buyers.

Step 2: Libraries License, They Don't Buy

Unlike print books, where a library buys a physical copy of a printed book, eBooks are licensed. That means the library pays to access your eBook for a set number of loans or a specific time period.

Some models include:

- One Copy/One User (OC/OU)
  (just like a print book, one loan at a time)
- Cost-per-Circulation (CPC)
  (library pays per checkout)

- Simultaneous Use (SU)
  (flat-fee access for unlimited users)

Important: Currently, most self-published eBooks are only available to libraries through the OC/OU or CPC model. That means your eBook won't appear in a library catalog until a reader requests it, and then the library pays a small fee if they lend it out.

So even if your eBook is "available" through OverDrive, it might not be visible in the catalog until someone asks for it.

Step 3: Set Your Library Pricing Carefully

When you publish your eBook through Draft2Digital or Kobo, you'll often be asked to set a library price that is completely separate from your regular eBook price. This is what the library sees when they consider licensing your title. If it's set too high, they'll skip it. If it's the same as your consumer price, you may not make much per loan.

Typical library pricing models:

- 2x or 3x your consumer price
- OR flat $9.99–$14.99 CAD for a full-length book
- Shorter titles or children's books can be lower (e.g., $4.99–$7.99)

Libraries are working with limited budgets, so keep it reasonable but don't undersell your work either (something that is very common for self-published authors, especially when they are first starting out).

Step 4: Promote Your eBook's Library Availability

Once your eBook is live and available for library licensing, it won't just magically appear in catalogs. You can:

- Let readers know they can request it at their local library
- Include a note in your author website or newsletter: *"Prefer to read through your library? My eBook is available on OverDrive just ask your librarian to request it by ISBN: [your ISBN]"*
- Use library-specific promo links from Kobo or D2D if available

Visibility doesn't always mean discoverability, sometimes you have to help readers (and librarians) find your eBook in the first place, just like for printed books.

Accessibility and EPUB Metadata

If you're creating an EPUB version of your book, take a moment to check its accessibility metadata. Platforms like Draft2Digital and InDesign allow you to include tags that describe your book's structure (headings, images, alt text), which can help screen readers navigate more easily. Tools like Ace by DAISY can scan your EPUB file and flag accessibility issues before distribution.

PLR and eBooks: Yes, They Count

If your eBook is held in a library collection, it may be eligible for the Public Lending Right (PLR) program in Canada, just like a print book.

But here's the catch, not all digital licenses count. The PLR office uses specific catalog databases to confirm that your eBook is available in participating libraries. If your book only exists in a "pay-per-loan" CPC model, and it hasn't been held in a library's official digital collection, it might not be found during the PLR sampling.

Still, it's worth registering your eBook in your PLR account if it meets the same eligibility as your print title. And, of course, it's always worth having your books in any form in a library!

Chapter 6: What About Audiobooks?

Audiobooks are growing in popularity, and yes Canadian libraries do license them. But the path is a bit murkier than with print or eBooks. There's no central vendor like Whitehots for audiobooks, and the platforms that libraries use are often locked behind distributor deals that don't include self-published authors by default.

Still, if you've produced an audiobook, it's worth understanding how to get it into Canadian libraries and, of course, what makes it eligible for PLR.

How Libraries Get Audiobooks

Most Canadian public libraries don't "buy" audiobooks the way they do physical books. Instead, they license them through digital lending platforms like OverDrive (Libby), Hoopla, and Bibliotheca. These systems allow libraries to offer temporary access, either one borrower at a time, or under a cost-per-checkout model.

But getting your audiobook into those systems isn't automatic. Libraries don't license from Audible or Amazon. If you've published your audiobook exclusively through ACX (Amazon's platform), it won't be available to libraries at all, and it won't qualify for PLR either.

How to Make Your Audiobook Available to Libraries

To get into library systems, you need to distribute your audiobook through a company that actually works with them. The two most accessible for indie authors right now are Findaway Voices (https://www.findawayvoices.com/) and Authors Republic (https://www.authorsrepublic.com/).

Both of these allow you to upload your audiobook files, set pricing specifically for library use, and opt into platforms like OverDrive, Hoopla, and Bibliotheca. Your book won't appear in every catalog automatically, but it will be available for libraries to license if they choose to.

Remember, if you've already gone exclusive with ACX, you'll need to wait out your term or remove the book from exclusivity to use these library-facing distributors.

Pricing and Discovery

When you upload your audiobook to a distributor like Findaway, you'll be asked to set both a retail and a library price. For libraries, your pricing should be competitive, too high and they won't license it, too low and you may not earn enough to make it worthwhile.

Even after you're listed, your audiobook may not be visible to libraries unless someone specifically requests it or it's surfaced through a recommendation. Letting your readers and listeners know they can ask their local library to license your audiobook can help it get discovered.

Audiobooks and PLR

Audiobooks are eligible for the Public Lending Right program if they meet the same basic criteria as print books in that they require a valid ISBN, are available in Canadian libraries, and published by a Canadian creator.

If your audiobook is only available through retail platforms like Audible or iTunes, it won't be found in PLR's sampling; however, if it's available through library systems like

Shelved

OverDrive, and libraries have actually added it to their collections, it can qualify.

When you register your audiobook inside your PLR account, choose "sound recording" as the format. You'll need to provide the ISBN and confirm that you're listed as a contributor.

Chapter 7: Getting Your Book Ready for Libraries

Before a library can buy your book, it has to meet certain professional standards. These aren't optional extras, they're how your book gets classified, shelved, and taken seriously by library buyers. This chapter covers the essentials: ISBNs, what self-publishers can and can't access through Library and Archives Canada, how to format your book, and what to include in your metadata.

ISBNs: The First Step to Being Discoverable

In Canada, we are very lucky because unlike in most other countries, like the United States, ISBNs are free through ISBN Canada. Don't forget, *you'll need a separate ISBN for each format of your book.* So if you have a paperback, hardcover, eBook, audiobook of one title, that would be four separate ISBN numbers.

When you apply, you'll be asked to create a publisher name. If you're self-publishing, this can be your own name, your imprint, it doesn't have to be a registered company, just something consistent. Using your own ISBNs (rather than free ones from Amazon) allows you to control how your book appears in databases and is essential if you want libraries to view your book as professionally published.

Preserving Your Book in the National Collection

Don't forget, while ISBNs are free for Canadian authors through Library and Archives Canada (LAC), using them comes with an obligation that once your book is published, you're required to submit one or more copies to LAC under legal deposit. This ensures your work is preserved as part of Canada's national collection.

You can find full details, including what to submit and where, on the official site:

https://library-archives.canada.ca/eng/services/legal-deposit/Pages/legal-deposit.aspx

Making Your Book Lendable Through LAC

When you submit your book to Library and Archives Canada (LAC) through the legal deposit, you're not just fulfilling a publishing obligation, you're ensuring your book is able to be *catalogued and discoverable* by libraries across the country.

Once accepted by the LAC, your book is added to Voilà, Canada's national union catalogue, which is part of the OCLC WorldCat system. This searchable record gives your book a professional presence that public, school, and academic librarians use when evaluating titles for acquisition.

Of course, the LAC legal deposit doesn't guarantee a spot on every shelf but it does put your book on the map. And for self-published authors, that visibility is a powerful first step toward getting borrowed and acquired by libraries.

CIP: Not Available for Self-Published Books

Cataloguing in Publication (CIP) is a program run by Library and Archives Canada that creates pre-publication cataloguing records. These include Dewey numbers, subject headings, and a block of text that libraries use to classify books.

But here's what you need to know, unfortunately, *self-published authors are not eligible for this program at this time.*

The CIP program only works with traditional publishers that publish a minimum number of titles per year *and* distribute through traditional channels. If you're using print-on-demand or publishing independently, your application will be rejected.

So while you won't have a CIP block on your copyright page, you can still make your book cataloguing-ready by using clear, accurate metadata, which brings us to the next section.

Trim Size and Format

Libraries are used to standard trim sizes. Sticking to common dimensions gives your book a better chance of being accepted and shelved properly. Of course, there are exceptions, but generally it is a good idea to pick a size that they are used to working with, if you haven't already published your book.

Examples of common book sizes found in libraries and available on popular print on demand sites:

- Paperback Fiction/Nonfiction:
  5.5" × 8.5" or 6" × 9"
- Children's picture books:
  8.5" × 8.5" (square) or 10" × 8" (horizontal)

Try to avoid spiral bindings, oversized books, or anything that looks like a workbook, unless that's your intended category. Always print books on quality paper, use professional cover and interior design, and choose durable binding formats *(especially for hardcover books)*.

One more thing to consider when preparing your book for libraries is accessibility. Most authors won't be able to meet every standard, but even small choices can improve how your book is experienced.

Thinking About Accessibility

Public libraries serve a wide range of readers including those who are differently-abled, have low vision, learning differences, or other access needs. While full accessibility isn't always possible for self-published authors, it's worth thinking about what you *can* do within your format and budget.

Here are a few considerations:

Large print editions

These aren't just for older adults; readers with vision impairment, neurodivergence, or cognitive disabilities may prefer them, too. A 16-point font minimum is standard. If your book is under 100 pages, a large print edition may help justify spine width for shelving.

Dyslexia-friendly fonts

Consider typefaces with clear letter differentiation (like Lexend or OpenDyslexic). Even using a well-spaced, sans-serif font like Verdana or Century Gothic can improve readability.

Alt-text for images (eBooks)

If you're producing an EPUB, include descriptive text for any illustrations or diagrams. This helps users with screen readers navigate the book meaningfully.

High-contrast design choices

Ensure that you haven't placed any text over busy backgrounds like images or tables, avoid low-contrast font colours (like pale grey on white).

These small decisions don't guarantee library adoption, but they do show a professional mindset and increase the chances your book will be usable by more readers. Even one change can make a difference, it's something to think about.

Helpful Tools for Accessible Self-Publishing

If you're interested in creating more inclusive books, these tools and resources are a great place to get some help.

Lexend Font Family (https://www.lexend.com/) Designed to improve reading fluency and reduce visual stress.

OpenDyslexic (https://opendyslexic.org/) A free, open-source font designed for readers with dyslexia.

BCALA's Print Guidelines

(**https://www.bcala.org/resources**)

Offers sample specs for creating large print editions.

Ace by DAISY - (https://inclusivepublishing.org/toolbox/ace-by-daisy-app/) A free tool that checks EPUB files for accessibility issues.

Google Docs' Built-In Accessibility Checker

Tools > Accessibility Useful for flagging heading structure or alt-text issues in drafts.

Adobe InDesign Accessibility Tools
https://helpx.adobe.com/indesign/using/creating-accessible-pdfs.html

If you're formatting your book professionally, InDesign can support tagged PDFs, alt-text, and more.

Remember, you don't need to do everything, even one or two improvements can make your book easier to use and more welcoming.

Metadata, BISAC and THEMA Codes

Metadata is what libraries see when they look up your book. This includes your title, subtitle, description, keywords, and subject categories.

One of the most important fields is your BISAC codes *(Book Industry Standards and Communications)*. These codes are a standardized subject category that tells distributors and library systems what your book is about.

As a self-published author, this is how you compensate for not having CIP data. You'll usually be asked to pick one to three

BISAC codes during setup (on platforms like IngramSpark or Draft2Digital). Choose carefully.

Using my first book, *Bye-Bye, Boobies* as an example, here are three appropriate BISAC codes for a weaning-themed children's picture book:

1. JUV039060 – Juvenile Fiction / Social Themes / Emotions & Feelings
2. JUV039050 – Juvenile Fiction / Social Themes / New Experience
3. JUV013070 – Juvenile Fiction / Family / New Baby

These reflect emotional transition, developmental change, and family structure without misclassifying the book.

Then, if I were to create a nonfiction parenting guide later about weaning, there is a breastfeeding-specific BISAC code under adult nonfiction:

- HEA041030 – Health & Fitness / Pregnancy & Childbirth / Breastfeeding

Shelved

But I wouldn't use that code for a picture book, even though it's about breastfeeding. It's a red flag for library systems expecting a juvenile fiction title, and likely it would be rejected by IngramSpark and other platforms if you tried to enter it in the metadata during the title review.

For this book, Shelved, again instead of defaulting to "General" categories or vaguely applicable publishing tags, I selected BISAC codes that align with both the content of this guide and the systems it's designed to help you navigate.

Primary:

LAN026000 – LANGUAGE ARTS & DISCIPLINES / Library & Information Science / Collection Development
Since this book focuses on how libraries acquire books, how public systems function, and how authors can navigate those processes. It directly addresses collection development workflows, making this BISAC a natural home.

Secondary:

LAN005000 – LANGUAGE ARTS & DISCIPLINES / Authorship
This book is a practical guide for self-published and

independently distributed creators who are managing their own metadata, marketing, and access to institutional systems.

Tertiary:
BUS043000 – BUSINESS & ECONOMICS / Small Business
  Since this book covers earnings, infrastructure, and income programs tied to public institutions, it aligns with creators who treat authorship as an independent business venture.

When choosing these codes, I passed on all "Writing Skills" or "Publishing / Reference" labels. This book isn't about how to write better or get traditionally published so those wouldn't apply. This book is about working with public institutions as a creator and getting paid.

Note on the word "General"

This book avoids vague top-level "General" BISAC codes such as *PUBLISHING / General* or *LANGUAGE ARTS / General* as they tend to bury books in broad, low-discoverability categories.

Subcategories like *Library & Information Science / General* can be more focused, but in this case, *Collection Development* offers a more precise match for the content. Specificity helps this book land on the shelves where creators, librarians, and educators are most likely to find and use it.

So, avoid picking *"General"* when it makes your book hard to find. Use it when it reflects a real, narrow domain like library science.

More About BISAC Codes

BISAC codes are used to categorize your book by subject, helping retailers, libraries, and distributors understand where it fits. You'll need to choose at least one BISAC code when publishing your book and ideally, the most specific one that applies.

These codes help determine shelving, search results, and even which vendor departments see your book. Choosing the wrong category (or something too broad) can make your book harder to find.

You can browse the full list of current BISAC codes here: https://bisg.org/page/BISACSubjectCodes

That web page includes a searchable spreadsheet and downloadable PDFs so you can find the best match for your title.

Codes are constantly added and deleted from this list, so be sure to check each time you publish a new book or a new version of a book to capture the ones that are currently in use.

More about THEMA Codes

While BISAC codes are the standard subject classification system for North American markets, international distributors often rely on THEMA codes, a globally recognized metadata system developed to serve book supply chains across multiple countries and languages.

If you plan to distribute your book through IngramSpark, international wholesalers, or global library systems, you may be asked to include one or more THEMA codes in addition to your BISAC classifications.

Like BISAC, THEMA codes categorize books by subject matter, but with slightly different terminology and structure. They also allow for qualifiers, such as region, language, or audience type, to support better discoverability in non-English or multilingual markets.

For example, a book like *Shelved* might use:

Primary: GBCR – Library and Information Services

Secondary: GBJ – Publishing and Book Trade, or KJVS – Small Business & Self-Employment

You can browse the full THEMA code list on their website (https://www.editeur.org/151/thema/).

If you're not distributing internationally right away, you don't need to choose THEMA codes today. But if you plan to publish through IngramSpark or target international libraries and bookstores, it's worth understanding how they work.

Writing a Library-Ready Description

Your book description isn't just marketing copy, it's your chance to show a librarian exactly where your book fits on the shelf. Keep it short, clear, and specific. Be sure to avoid vague phrasing like *"a must-have for any bookshelf"* or *"perfect for fans of...*" Instead, explain what the book does, who it's for, and what kind of collection it supports.

Example:

A gentle picture book about toddler weaning, told from the child's point of view. With comforting text and warm illustrations, it supports emotional literacy and family bonding. Created in Canadian English.

The back cover blurb can echo this language in a softer tone, but don't overdo it. Aim for sincerity over salesmanship. Most of the time you should keep it under 150 words.

What Is ONIX Metadata? (And Why You Probably Don't Need It)

If you're self-publishing through platforms like Amazon, Draft2Digital, or even IngramSpark, you'll enter your book's information title, author, description, BISAC codes, THERMA Codes, and keywords through their online forms. Behind the scenes, these platforms package your metadata into something called an ONIX file.

ONIX stands for Online Information Exchange, and it's the international standard for how books communicate with retailers, distributors, libraries, and metadata systems. It's a complex, XML-based format that can contain hundreds of data points beginning with our ISBN and page count to your cover image, pricing, and even author birth/death dates.

The good news? You don't need to create ONIX files yourself. Platforms generate them for you automatically. If you're managing your own ISBN block and working directly with distributors or large retailers, you might be asked to provide ONIX metadata, but most indie authors will never touch it directly.

Metadata Mistakes to Avoid

A strong book can still get overlooked if the metadata sends the wrong signals. Here are a few common missteps to avoid when preparing your title for library discovery.

Choosing the wrong BISAC code

If possible, don't default to "General" or grab the first keyword that sounds close. Inaccurate BISAC choices can misfile your book in unrelated categories or prevent it from being seen at all. It's worth taking the time to review the current codes (see link above) and have the best ones handy when you publish your book.

Mixing fiction and nonfiction categories

Using the same examples as before, if your book is a picture book, don't include parenting or health codes meant for adult nonfiction. It confuses systems and can block your book from juvenile listings.

Leaving fields blank

Distributors often ask for optional fields like age range, keywords, or subtitles and are often skipped over. Remember, those fields help libraries sort and find your book. Fill in everything you can, even if it's just one to two keywords.

Writing a vague description

Avoid fluffy language and overused phrases. Take some time to focus on what the book is, who it's for, and what role it could play in a library's collection.

Using Amazon-only language

Don't include Amazon bestseller claims, categories like "Kindle Short Read," or other retail jargon in your metadata. These mean nothing to libraries and often make the book look self-promotional. Save these for your website!

Not Perfect Metadata but the Right Metadata

Getting your metadata right doesn't require perfection but it does require thought. One of the best tips a librarian gave me, *"Try to think like a librarian: how would you know where to shelve this book if someone handed it to you?"*

Before you begin pitching, take a moment and make sure your book checks all the boxes in the Library-Ready Checklist (see Appendix E for the full list). It's an easy way to catch small issues like metadata mistakes or missing files before they become dealbreakers.

Chapter 8: The Truth About Platform-Issued ISBNs

Most Publishing Advice Isn't Written for Canadians

If you've looked online for tips on how to self-publish, you've probably come across blogs and videos that say, *"Just use the free ISBN Amazon gives you. It's faster and easier."* That advice might work for American and international authors, but it doesn't reflect how things work in Canada.

In Canada, ISBNs are free. You can register as a publisher with ISBN Canada and get as many as you need, at no cost. There's no need to rely on Amazon KDP, Draft2Digital, or other platforms to assign one for you, and for some people, doing so may limit what you can do later.

Who Is the Publisher?

When you accept a platform-issued ISBN, you are no longer listed as the publisher. The platform becomes the official publisher of record in the book's metadata, and your name or imprint is replaced with theirs. That metadata is what shows up in catalogues, library databases, grant applications, and anywhere your book is listed.

This isn't a problem if you're only publishing a private project or making eBooks for Kindle. But if you want your book to be taken seriously by Canadian institutions, or to qualify for government programs like PLR, then a platform-assigned ISBN is not the best choice.

Legal Deposit Isn't Guaranteed

Library and Archives Canada (LAC) expects books with ISBNs to be submitted through legal deposit. When your ISBN is issued by ISBN Canada and you're listed as the publisher, that process is straightforward. But when your ISBN belongs to Amazon or another American platform, LAC may reject the submission or reclassify the book as foreign-published.

Like all things, this doesn't happen in every case, some authors do get their books accepted with platform ISBNs but it's fair to say that it's unpredictable and you can't rely on it. If LAC doesn't accept your deposit, your book won't be listed in Voilà (Canada's national union catalogue), and it won't be included in WorldCat, either. That drastically reduces your discoverability in libraries.

PLR Eligibility Depends on Discoverability

The Public Lending Right program uses Canadian library catalogues to determine where books are held and who should be paid. If your book isn't found during the annual sampling process, it won't generate PLR income.

Platform ISBNs can interfere with this process. If you're not listed as the publisher, or if the book was never accepted by LAC for deposit, you may not appear in the catalogue data the PLR office uses. It's not just about whether your book is on a library shelf, it's about whether the system can find you correctly.

Libraries Don't Order from Amazon or Indigo

Another important point to remember, even if your book is listed on Amazon or Indigo, most Canadian libraries don't order from retail platforms. They buy through wholesalers and library distributors like Ingram, Whitehots, and B&T where they can get discounted prices. If your book isn't listed in those systems, or the metadata shows a platform publisher instead of you, your chances of being purchased are much lower.

Libraries prioritize books with clean metadata, proper cataloguing, and reliable fulfillment. Books that only exist on Amazon, or that appear to be self-published under Amazon's imprint, are often skipped over.

You Can Still Fix It

The good news is, if you've already published your book using a platform-issued ISBN, you're not stuck. You can create a brand new edition using a Canadian ISBN, update the copyright page to reflect your name or imprint, and re-release the book on the same platforms. From there, you can submit the new edition to LAC, get it listed in Voilà, and apply for PLR.

Plenty of Canadian authors make this switch once they realize what's at stake. Remember, it's not about chasing perfection, it's about building a long-term foundation that gives your book the best chance of being found, borrowed, and paid for.

Shelved

The Smart Choice for Canadian Authors

Using a free platform-issued ISBN might feel like an easy shortcut, but it often comes at the cost of discoverability, legitimacy, and income. If you want your book to be taken seriously by libraries, included in Canada's national collection, and considered for Public Lending Right payments, always use an ISBN from ISBN Canada.

It's free, it's yours, and it keeps you in control!

Chapter 9: PLR-Eligible Content vs. Library-Friendly

It's easy to assume that if your book qualifies for Canada's Public Lending Right (PLR), it must also be a book libraries want. After all, if it's eligible for government compensation, surely it belongs on the shelf, right?

Not quite. While there's overlap between PLR-eligible books and books libraries are willing to acquire or keep in circulation, the two categories aren't the same. And for many self-published authors, this gap is where expectations get quietly derailed.

If your goal is to be in libraries and also be eligible for the PLR funding, understanding the difference early can help you avoid wasting time registering titles that will never be found in a collection, and instead focus your efforts on creating books that are both fundable and findable.

Of course, if your goal is just to have your book in libraries, the PLR funding criteria isn't something you need to focus on at all.

What Makes a Book Eligible for PLR?

As mentioned in the previous chapters, you've seen the core PLR requirements *(the book must have a valid ISBN, be registered by someone who is eligible with a current account and, most importantly, it must be located in one of the program's surveyed Canadian public library systems to generate compensation).*

Unlike a publishing award or critical review, PLR registration is a technical process. It doesn't judge literary merit, artistic value, or writing skill. If your book qualifies on paper and turns up in a library collection, it counts regardless of how niche or unconventional it may be.

However, not all books make it through that first eligibility check.

Books That Don't Qualify for PLR but the Library Might Want Them

Even if a book has an ISBN and is sitting on your shelf, it may fall outside the program's scope. Below are some of the most common types of books that are explicitly ineligible for registration either because of format, content, or publishing arrangement.

Blank books, journals, planners, and notebooks

These include recipe logs, undated calendars, affirmation notebooks, or guided wellness prompts with minimal text. Even if they are beautifully designed, they don't meet the criteria for written literary or scholarly content. In some cases, libraries will include these in their collections.

Calendars and appointment books

Dated or undated, wall or desktop calendars are excluded in all forms. Libraries would also not be likely to add these to their shelves.

Books that contain no original Canadian writing

Translations or adaptations of non-Canadian works must include newly authored content by a Canadian citizen or permanent resident. A reprint of classic literature with a Canadian publisher's logo doesn't qualify on its own. While these don't qualify for the PLR, libraries will often include these in their collections.

Books published by vanity presses or services that list themselves as the author or rights holder

If the ISBN belongs to a company that is listed as the book's author or copyright owner *(e.g., some hybrid publishers or package-deal imprints)*, the author may not be considered eligible for PLR funding, even if they wrote the manuscript. Be sure to check with the company directly to understand if you can include the book in your PLR account. Libraries, of course, would consider books like this for their shelves.

Works where the author is anonymous, deceased, or only listed as an editor/translator without new writing

The PLR program requires a named, living Canadian author who contributed original content. Editing or compiling alone may not be sufficient when reviewed by the program. Generally speaking there is a 10% of content applied for the PLR grant. Libraries are happy to include these types of books if they feel that it matches their reader base.

Books not intended for general readership or literary use

Training manuals, corporate documents, internal reports, or technical binders generally fall outside the scope of PLR, even if they're bound and published. Some libraries will purchase books of this type, again depending on their reader base and type of library they are.

Titles presented solely as DVDs or apps

The PLR program currently supports print and recognized digital (eBook) as well as audio books. Video editions on their own are not accepted and neither are apps. Of course, libraries love DVDs and other types of lending materials so they make the perfect choice to market yours to.

Right now, f your book falls into any of these categories, it cannot be registered for the PLR program even if you find it in a library catalogue or it's sold through retail channels. Of course, this can change as time goes on so it's always better to check each year for any updates on types of things they are allowing to be registered.

Shelved

What Makes a Book Library-Friendly?

Even among PLR-eligible books, not all are library-friendly. Librarians aren't evaluating your title based on funding rules; they're considering their patrons, their space, and their collection development policies.

This means libraries are looking for books that are professionally presented, reasonably priced, and durable enough for circulation. Trim size, cover design, spine strength, and even the texture of the paper can influence whether a book is shelved or skipped. If the metadata is unclear, or if the book is only available from obscure vendors or without return options, it may be passed over entirely.

Having local or subject relevance helps, especially for children's books or nonfiction titles. But relevance alone won't be enough if the book doesn't hold up physically or look like it belongs on the shelf.

Why Some Books Qualify for PLR but Never Earn a Dime

A book can meet every PLR rule and still go nowhere, financially. In many cases, this happens because the book isn't in any of the libraries surveyed by the program. It may have been printed and registered, but never acquired by libraries. Or sometimes the book was acquired, but later weeded out or lost before the survey year.

This can happen for a variety of reasons. The book might be priced too high for its category, or printed with margins that make it physically unreadable. It might have metadata errors such as listing the author under one name on the cover and another in the database. Or it may be printed exclusively through Amazon without distribution to the suppliers libraries actually use.

All of these factors can keep a technically eligible book from being discovered during the annual PLR search and if it's not found, it doesn't get paid.

What About Donating Your Book?

Yes, you can donate a book to a public library and still receive PLR payments *if* the book is accepted into the collection and remains catalogued. That said, donation is never a guarantee of inclusion.

Many libraries have formal review processes for unsolicited donations. If the book doesn't meet their standards, in content, appearance, or format, it may be discarded, sold in a fundraiser bin, or quietly recycled. Even accepted books can be removed after a short trial period if circulation is low or damage occurs.

It's always worth contacting the library in advance and explaining why the book is relevant to their readers. If your book has local ties, curriculum applications, or a seasonal theme, those can increase the odds that it will be kept and counted.

Where These Paths Overlap

If you are planning on getting your book into libraries and applying for the PLR funding, the most strategic use of your time is creating books that meet both criteria from the start, books that are eligible for PLR *and* desirable to libraries.

This means that your book is:

- Well-formatted, durable, and clearly written for a target audience.

- Distributed through professional suppliers with fair pricing and returnability.
- Registered accurately with PLR and catalogued under a consistent author name and title.
- Relevant for at least one regional or topical reason that makes it valuable to a library.

There's no trick to this, just careful alignment. Think of it this way: PLR gives you the *potential* to be paid, but library readiness is what gets you *into the system* in the first place.

If You're Focused on Library Shelving but Not PLR

Not every author is aiming for PLR compensation, or even qualifies. Maybe you're more interested in visibility, community access, or simply knowing that your book is available in public spaces. Maybe your book is too old to be included before you found out about this program but you still want it to be in libraries for people to have access. That's a completely valid goal and in many ways, the path to library shelving follows the same advice.

Shelved

You'll still want professional formatting, clean metadata, a reasonable price point, and distribution through channels libraries already use. Those factors make or break acquisitions. But if your book isn't eligible for PLR because of format, publishing method, age, or creator status it doesn't mean you can't get it onto library shelves. It just means you won't receive government payments if it's borrowed.

Plenty of authors choose this route. They donate copies to local branches, pitch directly to selectors, or position their book around a community theme. It may take more legwork and, like all books, there's no guarantee the book will stay in circulation long term, but the opportunity is still there.

Whether or not you register for PLR, being in a public library is a powerful form of access. You're giving your readers a no-barrier way to find your work and for most authors, that's priceless.

Chapter 10: Who Qualifies for the PLR Program

Registering a book is only part of the process to receive payments through the PLR Program, you also need to qualify as a creator. That means you contributed meaningful content to the book, and your name appears in the published record.

This chapter breaks down which roles are eligible including authors, illustrators, editors, translators, and more and what kinds of contributions meet the program's minimum threshold. Whether you created a picture book, co-edited an anthology, or translated a nonfiction title, it's important to understand how eligibility works, how shares are divided, and what disqualifies a contributor from receiving funding.

In addition to format and genre exclusions, PLR also looks at the creator's contribution. Just because your name is listed in the book doesn't automatically mean you'll be eligible for payment. You need to have contributed enough original content to meet the program's minimum threshold.

Authors and Editors

For PLR purposes, a creator must have contributed at least 10 pages and 10% of the total book but the way that's measured depends on the type of book.

It's easy to calculate for standard books, by page count.

But in children's books, graphic novels, and other illustrated works, the program evaluates contribution based on word count, since many pages may include little or no text.

Eligible content includes prefaces, afterwords, chapter text, or other original written work, not things like contributor bios, indices, dedications, or captions with no narrative function.

For example, if you're a co-author who added a few lines of dialogue or an illustrator who also wrote a handful of rhyming labels, that may not be enough to qualify. But if you wrote the text of a 32-page picture book, even if the word count is short, you're almost certainly eligible.

Editors can also qualify if they contribute at least 10% of the book's content in writing. A sole editor may claim 20% of the payment; two editors can split it at 10% each, provided they both meet the writing threshold.

This rule is especially important when multiple creators are involved. If your role is primarily visual or structural, you may not be eligible unless you've also written enough content to meet the criteria.

What About Illustrators?

If you're the illustrator of a book, you can register for PLR and receive payments, even if you didn't write a single word. This is especially relevant for picture books, graphic novels, and illustrated nonfiction. As long as your name is properly credited in the book as the illustrator (on the cover, title page, or formal metadata), your artistic contribution counts.

You do not need to meet a minimum page or word count, and there's no additional content requirement like there is for editors or contributors. The illustrations themselves are considered eligible creative work.

If you co-illustrated a book with someone else, the payment will be split evenly between all credited illustrators.

Illustrators using stock art, or whose work was omitted from the official metadata, will not qualify. If you created the art but aren't named anywhere in the published edition, the PLR office cannot include you.

Other Contributors Who May Qualify

While the most common claimants are authors and illustrators, there are other creative contributors who can also qualify for PLR as long as they meet the content threshold and are formally credited in the book. These include the following types of contributors.

Translators

If you translated the book into English or French and your name is formally credited as the translator, you may be eligible to register. The translation must represent a significant intellectual contribution not just light editing or adaptation. PLR payments to translators follow the same 10% minimum content rule and are typically capped at a set share (e.g., 50% shared between translator and original author unless otherwise declared).

Photographers

In photographic books, such as nonfiction titles, historical albums, or art monographs, a credited photographer may be eligible, particularly if the photography is central to the book and not just decorative. They must be listed by name and not just included in a blanket "photo credits" section.

Cartographers

In books where original maps are a core feature like atlases, regional guides, or educational nonfiction, a credited cartographer may be eligible if their creative contribution is substantial and clearly attributed.

Designers or Visual Creators *(in rare cases)*

If the designer's role goes beyond layout or typesetting and includes original artistic or visual work central to the book's purpose, and they are credited, they may qualify. This is more likely in books where the designer is effectively a co-creator, such as concept books or experimental visual works.

Chapter 11: Building Your Outreach Toolkit

When I first started looking into how to get my book into the local library, I assumed I could simply walk in and donate a copy. I thought I was doing them a favour, one less book to buy, right? But it turns out that most libraries don't appreciate unsolicited donations. In fact, if a book arrives without a formal request or proper approval, it often ends up in the fundraising bin, rather than on the shelf.

Thankfully, my library was clear, they *do* support local authors, and they have a designated section for them. But I couldn't just email someone or hand over a copy. I had to fill out a submission form, follow the process, and wait.

That's when I realized just how important it is to plan your library outreach like a professional. This chapter walks you through how to do exactly that; whether you're sending emails or filling out forms, building your own spreadsheet, or waiting for mine to be ready. With a bit of structure, you can stop guessing and start getting your book into the right hands.

Shelved

Why a Spreadsheet Matters (Even a Simple One)

Library outreach can feel chaotic very quickly if you don't have a system. A spreadsheet helps you track:

- Who you contacted
- How you contacted them (email, form, in-person)
- What they said (or didn't say)
- When to follow up

You don't need to build it all at once. Start with your home province, or even just your local system. Ten quality contacts will serve you better than a vague list of two hundred.

How to Build Your Own Contact List

Start small. Pick one province or region and aim for 10–15 libraries, the closest ones to you first as you are not just a Canadian author, you are a local one!

Use the national library directory to begin your search

The Government of Canada website provides a searchable directory of Canadian libraries and their system codes. It's a great way to identify library systems by province or city and where I started with my library outreach plan.

Search for staff directories or contact pages

Once you have narrowed down your top libraries, visit each library system's website. Look for staff listings under "Contact," "About Us," or "Collection Development." If an email is available, add it to your spreadsheet.

Check for submission forms

Many libraries now prefer "Suggest a Title" forms instead of emails. These connect directly with acquisitions teams and are often required for local author books.

Record what you find in a spreadsheet

For each library, track the following:

- Library system name
- Branch (if applicable)
- Contact name and email or "submission form only"
- Mailing Address
- Province or territory

- Acquisition method (e.g., centralized, accepts indie books, form only)
- Date contacted
- Response received or follow-up needed

This isn't just admin work. It's how you turn one-off efforts into a sustainable system.

Submitting via Forms: What to Expect

Many libraries will not consider a book unless it's submitted through their form. That was the case with my own local system. No cold emails. No drop-offs. Just a structured, quiet gatekeeping system.

These forms usually ask for:

- Your book's title and author
- ISBN and format (e.g., paperback, hardcover, eBook)
- Audience (e.g., toddlers, teens, general adult readership)
- A short description or marketing blurb
- The reason the book might interest their community

Some forms even let you attach a PDF sample or include links to reviews.

Here's a general example of what you can include in the "Why this title should be added" or "Additional Comments" box:

I'm a Canadian author based in Ontario, and this title has been well received by families looking for gentle weaning stories. It's available through IngramSpark and aligns with themes already present in your children's collection. The book includes Canadian imagery and supports Canadian Public Lending Rights registration.

Keep it professional and direct, this isn't the place to over explain or push. Think of it as the back cover pitch, plus a short note on relevance.

A Note on Outcomes (and Uncertainty)

Even when you follow all the steps and submit a form correctly, there's no guarantee your book will be added. Some libraries will email you if your title is approved. Others won't reply at all; they may quietly purchase it, or quietly pass.

With limited budgets and thousands of requests, many libraries leave it to the author to check the catalogue later. That's normal. It doesn't mean your book was ignored but it does mean *you* have to do the follow-up. This is where the spreadsheet dates help a lot.

Some systems will confirm if they've added your book and even let you drop off a physical copy after approval. Others will only purchase directly through Ingram or a distributor, and they'll let you know if your title isn't available through the channels they use.

This variation is exactly why your spreadsheet matters. It helps you stay on top of where things stand without letting anything slip through the cracks.

When Direct Emails Work Better

Not every library uses forms. Some, especially smaller or rural branches, still accept email suggestions directly. In these cases, a short, customized email works best. Be sure that you include:

- A greeting with the librarian's name (if available)

- Your book title, ISBN, format, and a 1–2 sentence description max
- A note on relevance Canadian content, local interest, or topic fit
- A link to your Ingram listing or website
- A friendly closing, such as: *"If this title is of interest, I'd be happy to provide more info or send a review copy."*

Be respectful, concise, and professional. And don't be discouraged by silence; many libraries will order the book without replying at all.

How Many Follow-Ups Is Too Many?

One follow-up is considered standard, two at most. If you haven't heard back after four to six weeks, it's fine to send a short, polite message asking if they had a chance to review your submission. A second follow-up is only appropriate if you're offering new information *(like updated distribution)* or clarifying a partial response. Beyond that, it's best to move on. Many libraries won't reply unless they're adding your book, and silence often just means "not right now." Don't get discouraged!

Again, this is where the spreadsheet can come in handy once you've submitted your book, add a follow up date for the future so that you can keep track of those too.

Remember, start small. Reach out to one library a week, start with your local library then the one the next town or city over. Fill out one form, send one email, add one row to your own spreadsheet. This isn't about being everywhere at once, it's about being thoughtful, persistent, and prepared.

That's how books get on public shelves.

Chapter 12: Writing Your Pitch

Pitching your book to a library is not about asking for a favour. It's about making a thoughtful, professional offer that helps a librarian serve their community better. Your email isn't a marketing blast, and it's not a personal plea. It's a short, specific introduction to your book, framed around what libraries actually care about: usefulness, relevance, and accessibility.

If that sounds transactional, it's because it is. A good pitch respects the librarian's time, shows you've done your homework, and makes it easy for them to take the next step of accepting your book.

Be Clear, Not Clingy

Most library staff are overworked, underpaid, and drowning in emails. What they need is clarity and definitely not a rambling message about your publishing journey, and one that is using a desperate tone.

The worst thing you can do is open your pitch with something like:

"I know I'm just a self-published author, but..."

or

"I really need help getting the word out..."

That might feel humble to you, but to a librarian, it sounds like extra work and low quality control. Don't downplay your book. Stand behind it.

You can (and should) still be friendly. But don't be apologetic. If your book is professional, returnable, and relevant, then it belongs in the collection. Your email just needs to show that.

What Libraries Actually Want to Know

Your pitch email should answer these questions quickly:

- What is the book, and who is it for?
- Why should our library consider it?
- Is it available through standard acquisition channels (Ingram, etc.)?

- Can we return it if needed?
- Does it qualify for PLR? (optional - only if that is something important to you to share)
- Where can we read more or preview it?

That's it. You don't need a full press kit or a marketing campaign. Most libraries want a clean paragraph, a link, and the option to ask for more. Anything beyond that is usually overkill.

If your book is regionally relevant (e.g., set in your province, features Canadian content, tackles a local theme), say so clearly and early. Local relevance is one of the strongest reasons a library will consider a title, especially if it's also professionally presented and available from their preferred distributors.

Sample Email Template

Subject line: Local children's book on toddler weaning

Dear [Librarian's Name],

I'm a local author, illustrator and International Board Certified Lactation Consultant based in [Your Town]. I recently published a picture book titled Bye-Bye, Boobies, which helps families navigate toddler weaning in a gentle, age-appropriate way. The book is set in a Canadian context, with subtle regional elements, like Canadian plaid blankets, maple leaves, and our familiar wildlife. It's designed to reflect real parenting experiences, including breastfeeding beyond infancy.

The book is available through IngramSpark (returnable with standard trade discount) and qualifies for the Public Lending Right program.

I've included a link to the book's information page here: [insert link]

I'd be happy to provide a review copy or answer any questions. Thank you for considering it for your collection.

Warm regards,

[Your Name]
[Your Website or Linktree]
[Optional: Phone number or mailing address]

This can be adapted to any genre, of course. The key is that it's short, informative, and clearly shows why your book is a good fit.

What Not to Say in your Pitch

There's a particular kind of pitch that instantly gets a hard pass. It's the kind that centers the author's struggles instead of the book's usefulness.

Some phrases to avoid in an email:

- "I'm just an indie author looking for a chance…"
- "Please help me get my book out there…"
- "I know this isn't professionally published, but…"
- "Can I drop off a copy at your branch?"

These don't position your book as a valuable resource. They frame the librarian as a gatekeeper with the power to validate your work and that's not how this relationship works.

Librarians want to help, but they're not running a mentorship program. They need to know whether your book is useful to their patrons, affordable for their budget, and easy to order through their systems.

Should You Offer a Free Copy to the Library?

If your book is over $25 or you're pitching to dozens of libraries, it's okay to hold back on this one. That being said, you should still be prepared to send a review copy if asked. This is standard practice. Most librarians won't ask unless they're seriously considering your book, but it helps to signal that you're open to it.

If you *are* mailing copies to libraries to add to their collection, don't do it cold. Ask first and send the book along with a personal cover letter to the person you spoke to and who has confirmed that they want a copy of your book for their collection. These days many libraries are moving away from physical review copies because of storage issues and donation policies.

Based on countless conversations with authors in Canada and the U.S., I can't stress this enough, don't frame your book drop-off as a "gift." It may end up in the donation bin, unprocessed and unread. Always email first and get the name of the person who wants to review the book, mark the envelope to their attention with a personal note, before sending a book.

Tone and Timing

When in doubt, aim for professional but warm. Use plain language. Avoid exclamation marks, emojis, over-sharing, or "inspirational" talk. This isn't your back cover blurb on a book. You're writing to a peer in the information sector, not a potential reader.

Following Up

As mentioned before, if you don't hear back from your initial contact with the library after four to six weeks, a single follow-up is fine. Keep it brief, and don't send a guilt trip. If you still don't hear anything, move on to the next contact on your list and make a note in your spreadsheet.

One thing that I've discovered is that libraries often plan purchases months in advance or pass titles around for committee review and, of course, not every pitch will land, and not every book fits every collection. That doesn't mean your book isn't worth reading, it just means you're building a longer path into the library world, one relationship and one email at a time.

Keep your spreadsheet updated, stay professional, and remember: Persistence works best when it's paired with respect.

Chapter 13: If You're Credited, You Count: Tips for Non-Author Creators

Many books are a team effort and yet, in most publishing conversations, only the author gets mentioned. But if your name appears anywhere in the credits on the cover, the title page, or even the copyright page you should be included as a creator.

This chapter is for everyone who has contributed meaningfully to a published book but isn't the author. That includes:

- Illustrators and cover artists
- Photographers
- Translators
- Editors (where named)
- Designers, layout artists, typographers
- Contributing writers or creators of supplementary content

If your name appears as an official credit in the book, you can play a role in getting it into libraries and potentially get paid for your contribution through Canada's Public Lending Right program (PLR), but it starts with visibility.

Libraries Care About the Book, Not Who Sends It

Libraries don't vet submissions based on who mails the book or who sends the pitch email. They look at:

- The book's quality and relevance
- The metadata and catalog information
- Whether the book fits a gap or supports a need in their collection

That means if the author hasn't submitted the book or doesn't plan to, you, as the credited creator, can. You don't need to own the copyright, and you don't need to speak on the author's behalf. You're simply helping the book find its place.

As a general rule, libraries receive and review thousands of titles every year. Being proactive, especially if you have a local connection or unique artistic angle, can help the book stand out, sometimes even better than the author.

You Can Be the One to Reach Out to Libraries

If you're the illustrator, translator, photographer, or other named contributor, and especially if you live in the region of the library you're contacting, you can write directly, like in the example below.

Sample Outreach Email for Non-Author Contributors

Subject: Book Submission: [Book Title] – Illustrated by a Local Creator

Dear [Librarian's Name or Library Team],

I'm reaching out as the [illustrator/photographer/translator] of a recently published book titled [Book Title] by [Author Name]. It was published in [Year] and is currently available through [distribution method or ISBN info, e.g. IngramSpark, ISBN 978-1-234567-89-0].

I'm based in [City/Province], and I thought it might be a good fit for your collection, especially as a locally connected or independently produced title. I'd be happy to donate a copy or send more information if needed.

Thank you for your time and for supporting Canadian creators.

Sincerely,

[Your Full Name]

[Role in the Book, e.g. Illustrator]

[Optional: Website or Portfolio Link]

This email is short, respectful, and clear about your role without overstepping the author's position. It leaves the door open for a donation or further information, and it reinforces your connection to the local area which can carry weight in library acquisitions.

This simple outreach is often more than enough. If the library is interested, they'll let you know how to proceed and if the author never planned to do this step, you've just given the book a chance it would have missed.

Often, authors are happy to provide copies of their books if you ask for them at little or no cost to you, especially for places like libraries. If a library asks for a copy to be provided, be sure to check to see if the author can help here vs buying the book at the retail price. Authors usually can purchase their books at a discounted price or some might have copies on hand that they are using for in-person shows.

Why It's Worth Doing

Even if the book isn't yours alone, getting it into libraries helps in lots of ways:

- Your professional reputation. Libraries lend for years, and many keep contributor names in their records.
- Future collaborations. Authors and publishers notice when illustrators take initiative.
- Your eligibility for the PLR program. If the book ends up in Canadian libraries and your name is listed, you may qualify for payments.

How PLR Applies to You

The Public Lending Right program allows non-author contributors to claim a percentage share of payment for any book they're credited in as long as the book is found in eligible Canadian public libraries.

You must:

- Be personally named in the book (not a studio or business)
- Have a verifiable contribution (e.g., art, translation, photos)
- Be a Canadian citizen or permanent resident with an open PLR account
- Register the book during the open PLR claim window (usually February–May)

If the author also claims the title, you'll be asked to agree on a percentage split (which can be done online). If they don't register, you can still claim your share; you just won't get 100% of the payment unless you're the sole registered contributor.

It all starts with visibility and getting the book into library collections is the first step.

Take the Initiative

In creative work, especially in children's books and translations, the non-author contribution is often just as important to a book's success. But unless someone takes the time to get the book into catalogues, libraries, and official systems, it may quietly disappear.

If the author is too overwhelmed, too modest, or just not interested in library outreach, don't assume that nothing can be done. You can help and you can benefit. You might be surprised how much the author appreciates this once you confirm the book is on the shelves.

Chapter 14: Timing Your Pitch and When to Follow-Up

Once you've written your pitch and built a contact list, the next challenge is how and when to actually reach out. Pitching libraries isn't a one-time blast. It's a long game that depends heavily on timing, pacing, and persistence. This chapter covers when to contact libraries based on their seasonal patterns, how to follow up without becoming a nuisance, and how to manage your outreach in a way that won't eat up your entire life.

Understanding Library Timing Cycles

Library purchasing isn't random; it runs on budget cycles, programming calendars, and internal review processes. If you send your pitch during a dead zone, it might not get seen at all. But if you time it right, your book could land on someone's acquisitions desk right as they're preparing their next order.

Most public libraries operate on either a calendar fiscal year (January to December) or a government cycle that starts in April. That means early winter through late spring is often the best window for initial outreach.

In January, many systems are starting fresh budgets and planning purchases for the year. In February and March, leftover funds may still be available from the previous year. By spring, some librarians are building lists for summer and fall programming, and may be more receptive to new titles.

Summer

Summer can be hit or miss. Some staff go on vacation. Some budgets freeze. Others spend the quiet season evaluating which new releases to bring in before fall begins. If you pitch in the summer, you may not get a quick response but you might catch someone who finally has time to read emails and review recommendations. The key is not to expect urgency. Libraries move slowly, but they do move.

Late Summer/Early Fall

By August and September, things begin to pick up again. School-year programs restart, staff return, and new acquisitions often resume. This is a good time to send a second wave of emails if your book came out earlier in the year and you haven't yet followed up. If your book has educational, parenting, or seasonal relevance, this is also your moment to highlight it. Many libraries make fall purchases with holiday displays or year-end funding in mind.

Late Fall

Late fall, especially November and December, is typically a lull. Some libraries shut down purchases entirely during this time. Others are scrambling to spend their remaining budget before it expires. It's unpredictable. Unless you're specifically told otherwise, it's better to avoid first-time outreach in December. Use that time to regroup and plan your next round of emails for January, when inboxes clear and new purchasing windows reopen.

How Long to Wait Before Following Up

If you send an email and don't get a reply, you're not alone. Libraries are swamped, and they don't have time to respond to every author. Silence doesn't mean your book was rejected and it doesn't mean you should give up, either.

As a general rule, wait about four to six weeks after your initial pitch before sending a follow-up. This gives staff time to read, flag, and discuss submissions, especially in larger systems where acquisitions decisions go through multiple people. If you pitched during a slower time of year, like summer or the December holidays, you might stretch that to seven or eight weeks just to account for delays.

Your first follow-up should be short, respectful, and direct. A polite nudge that references your original message and thanks them for their time is all you need. Don't resend the entire pitch or try to pressure them. You're just bringing your book back to the top of their inbox.

If another month goes by after you have sent that initial follow-up and you still haven't heard anything, it's okay to send one last check-in. This is especially worth doing if something notable has changed. For example, your book was reviewed, featured in a local paper, added to another library system, or selected for a school program. Those are gentle ways to reframe your offer without feeling like you're just repeating yourself.

After two follow-ups, it's best to let it go. If they're interested, they'll find a way to order your book. If not, move on to the next library on your list. You can always come back next year, especially if you've released a new edition or launched a follow-up title.

Sample Follow-Up Email (After No Response)

Subject: Follow-Up: [Your Book Title] Submission

Dear [Librarian's Name],

I hope this message finds you well. I wanted to follow up on my previous email regarding my book [Book Title], which I submitted for consideration in [Month].

It's a Canadian-authored title available through IngramSpark (returnable with standard terms), and I thought it might be a good fit for your collection. I'm happy to provide any additional information or a review copy if helpful.

Thank you again for your time, and I appreciate all the work you do supporting local readers and authors.

Warm regards,
[Your Name]
[Your Website or Linktree]
[Optional: ISBN again for convenience]

Sample Follow-Up Email (After Submitting Through a Form)

Subject: Follow-Up on Submitted Title – [Your Book Title]

Dear [Library Name] Team,

I recently submitted [Book Title] through your online Suggest-a-Title form and wanted to follow up in case any additional information would be helpful.

It's a Canadian-created [format, e.g. picture book / nonfiction title], available through IngramSpark (returnable, with standard library terms). If you'd like a review copy or ISBN confirmation, I'd be happy to provide that.

Thank you for considering the title, and for supporting Canadian creators through your collection choices.

Warmly,
[Your Name]
[Optional: ISBN]
[Optional: Website or contact info]

Shelved

Keeping Track Without Losing Steam

Outreach doesn't need to become your part-time job but it does require structure. If you're sending emails without logging who you contacted, when, or how they responded, it's easy to get overwhelmed or send duplicates.

Your spreadsheet is your best friend here. Start by logging the basics: Library name, contact email, region, and the date you sent your first pitch. When you send a follow-up, add that date too. If you get a reply, whether it's a "yes," "no," or "we'll consider it", make a note.

Some authors also track things like estimated order timelines, who handles acquisitions at each branch, or whether their title has shown up in the catalogue yet. Do what works for you. The goal is to stay organized without making the spreadsheet a second career.

Set realistic goals for yourself. You don't need to email fifty libraries in a day. In fact, spacing things out will help you manage replies and follow-ups more easily. A small weekly batch of say, five to ten emails is more than enough to keep the momentum going. Plus, it gives you time to personalize messages if you're writing to specific communities, librarians you've met, or systems where your book has a natural fit.

By keeping the process light, repeatable, and grounded in your schedule, you'll avoid burnout. Outreach isn't a one-and-done task, it's something you'll return to over time, especially as your backlist grows.

You don't need to pitch every library on your list today. You just need to keep your book in motion, one small wave at a time.

Chapter 15: How and When to Apply for the PLR Program in Canada

If you're ready to apply to the Public Lending Right (PLR) program, this chapter will walk you through exactly how to do it and how to avoid common mistakes that could get your book rejected. Even though it's a federal program, Canada Council's PLR system isn't overly complicated once you know where to go and what to enter.

We'll also touch on a few lesser-known income programs for authors in British Columbia, Ontario, and elsewhere.

Who Can Apply?

To be eligible for the Public Lending Right (PLR) program in Canada, you must be a living Canadian citizen or permanent resident, and be credited by name in the book as an eligible contributor (author, illustrator, translator, etc.)

If you live outside of Canada but still hold Canadian citizenship or permanent residency, you're still eligible to register, as long as your other contributor details match.

When to Apply

The PLR program opens for new registrations once a year, typically from *mid-February to mid-May.* You must submit your eligible titles during this window, at this time, there are no late submissions. If you miss the deadline, you'll have to wait until next year's cycle.

Each contributor may register up to 20 new titles per year, with a maximum of 25 active titles in your contributor file at any given time. Titles are retired automatically after 25 years or after five consecutive years of not being found in the annual PLR library sampling.

Important to remember, you don't have to wait for your book to appear in libraries before registering. As long as the book is published and meets the eligibility criteria, it's worth adding it during the registration window in case libraries acquire it later. These days, libraries often do not confirm that they have added titles to their collections.

Where to Register for the PLR Program

The PLR system is managed by the Canada Council for the Arts. You'll submit your registration online here:

https://publiclendingright.ca/registration-process

To complete your first registration, you'll need:

- Your contact information
- A Canadian SIN and bank account
- A scan or digital photo of the title page and copyright page
- The ISBN, publisher, and year of publication - titles accepted must have been published within the past five years
- Your contributor role (author, illustrator, translator, etc.)

Each eligible contributor must create their own account and register their own claim. For example, if a book has both an author and an illustrator, each person registers separately, with the same ISBN and copyright information/images, to claim their share of the payment.

Shelved

Step-by-Step Walkthrough

1. **Create or Log In to Your Account**

   Go to:

   https://publiclendingright.ca/registration-process

   and click "Register or Login." If this is your first time, follow the prompts to set up a contributor account.

2. **Enter Contributor Details**

   Confirm your role and name exactly as it appears in your book.
   Important to note, if you use a pen name or have changed your name, you may be asked to provide documentation by the program administrators.

3. **Add a New Title**

   Select "Register a Title." Fill in the ISBN, title, publisher, year, and format (print, eBook, audio). Upload the required pages (normally the title and copyright pages but this can change be sure to follow the instructions at the time).

4. **Claim Your Role**

   Choose your contributor type (e.g. primary author, co-illustrator) and specify your share of contribution. If there are multiple contributors for a single role, the payment is divided amongst all of the contributors.

5. **Submit and Track**

   Your registered title will appear in your contributor file. You can check back annually to update titles and view your payment statement.

Common Mistakes to Avoid with the PLR Program

Here are some of the most frequent reasons titles get rejected or flagged.

Uploading the wrong pages

Do not upload the front cover of the book. You must include a clear image of the title page and copyright page only.

Registering too early

The book you are registering must be published (not just written or pre-ordered) before you register.

Name or role doesn't match

If your name isn't listed in the book, or you're not credited in a qualifying role, your registration may be declined.

Ineligible contributor types

In most cases editors, layout designers, and cover artists are not eligible unless they also authored or illustrated the main content.

Missing the registration window

PLR registration only happens once a year. There is no grace period or late filing option.

Are PLR Payments Taxable?

Yes all PLR payments are considered taxable income in Canada, regardless of the amount. If you receive $500 or more in a calendar year, the Canada Council for the Arts will issue a T4A slip. This slip is used to report the income on your tax return, typically under self-employment or other income.

If your payment is under $500, you may not receive a T4A from them, but you are still required to report the income. So be sure to keep your annual PLR statement for your records and include it when filing your taxes.

This is why you'll need to provide a valid Canadian SIN when you register for the PLR Program, and all payments are made by direct deposit into a Canadian bank account.

Does PLR Count Against Grant Limits?

No. PLR payments are considered income which are completely separate from grants. They do not count against Canada Council grant totals and will not affect your eligibility or standing with any other project-based or career development funding.

PLR is not a grant, it's a payment for the presence of your work in public libraries. You can receive both PLR income and Canada Council or provincial grants in the same year without penalty.

Other Programs: Provincial Equivalents and Alternatives

Although the PLR program is federal, some provinces offer additional support for authors, and other creators, including grants, appearance fees, and professional development funding. While there are no other provincial PLR programs, nearly every province and territory in Canada has some form of project or professional development funding that literary artists can access.

I've included an entire chapter for these later in the book.

Don't Forget to Reapply for the PLR Each Calendar Year

Registering your title once isn't enough; you must return to the PLR system every year during the application window, even if you're not adding any new titles.

The annual registration window (mid-February to mid-May) is also your chance to:

- Update your contributor file
- Register any new books
- Confirm existing titles are still active
- Ensure your banking info is current

The Canada Council does not remind you to do this. It is entirely your responsibility to track the registration window and reapply each year. If you forget, your books won't be counted in that year's library survey and you may miss out on payments even if your book is sitting on shelves.

So be sure to set a recurring calendar reminder, or add it to your annual publishing checklist. Showing up once a year is the only way to keep your file active and eligible for compensation.

PLR won't make you rich, but it's a meaningful way to be recognized and compensated for your contribution to Canadian public culture. Once you're set up, all you have to do is show up once a year and keep creating.

Let libraries do the rest.

Chapter 16: Leveraging Your Library Success

You did it! Your book is in a library. Maybe it's just one, maybe it's a dozen, maybe more. Regardless of the number, that library shelf is more than just a spot to rest your book's spine. It's proof that your work has value, that it passed through selection criteria, and that someone, most often a trained librarian with limited shelf space, decided it was worth adding to a public collection. That's not just a win, it's a tool, and something to be proud of.

Tracking Your Book's Presence in Libraries

Going back to your spreadsheet, start by tracking where your book has landed. This isn't just for ego, although, let's be honest, it feels amazing, it's for data.

Since libraries often do not share with contributors that they have added your work to their collections directly these days, these two powerful tools can help you track.

WorldCat - https://www.worldcat.org/

This global catalog aggregates listings from over 10,000 libraries worldwide. Search by your name, ISBN, or title and keep track of which libraries have picked it up.

Individual library catalogues

There are still many libraries that aren't part of WorldCat or take time to sync. Use Google searches like "[Your Book Title]" site:yourlibrarydomain.ca to check local listings that may not show up right away.

One thing I'd recommend you do is save screenshots or links as you go. Not only does this help with future marketing or grant applications, but it's also a backup if a library ever removes the title and it disappears from the catalogue.

If you notice your book being held in a major city system, or in multiple provinces or states, that's worth highlighting. A single academic library carrying your book on parenting or the creative process can add major credibility. If a small-town library has added multiple books from your series, that's a sign you're resonating with real families. This is all useful data, both to you and to potential readers.

Often libraries welcome creators into their spaces as a way to share their work, so when you see your books in a library close to you (or further away if you can get there) reach out and ask if you can come in for a reading or a book signing.

Using Library Placements in Your Marketing

Library placement can feel quiet, there's no flashy "launch day" or box of sales receipts. But it can be incredibly persuasive to readers. When you post about your book on social media or on your website, include a line like:

"Now available in libraries across Canada, be sure to ask your local branch to request it!"

Better yet, name a few specific cities or systems:

"You can now borrow my book at your local library in Toronto, Vancouver, Winnipeg, and more."

It doesn't come across as bragging, it reads as trust. Readers are more likely to explore a book they know has been vetted by professionals.

If you're running ads, adding a line like *"Also available in public libraries"* (especially in a carousel with Amazon or retailer links) can improve conversions. Some readers are on the fence, not because of cost, but because they're unsure if your book is a *real* book. Library placement can help shift that perception.

Don't forget to include this in your author bio, your media kit, and even your press releases:

"Her work is held in public libraries across five provinces."

It tells people you're serious. That your book has staying power. And that it's not just a print-on-demand product with no footprint.

Long-Term Value of a Backlist

One of the most overlooked benefits of getting into libraries is what it can mean for your backlist. Even if your sales have

Shelved

slowed down or you've moved on to newer titles, libraries can keep older books in circulation for years, order books multiple copies that are in high demand, or when one is damaged, and that all has an impact on the PLR.

If a book remains on shelves and continues to be borrowed or discovered, it may keep generating Public Lending Right income long after you've stopped actively marketing it, up to 25 years! That's passive income, but only if the title stays visible.

You can help by checking in once or twice a year to see if your book is still in library systems. If it's gone missing from a catalogue, consider whether to reach out or try another branch. If it's still there, celebrate that quietly and keep it in mind when planning future outreach, you may want to release a new edition or companion title that revives interest in the first.

Have a new book or adding a second book in a series? Libraries who already bought the first are much more likely to consider the next which is why it is important to track who has your books as you can start with those ones when you pitch your newest work. This is exactly why that spreadsheet that you've got comes in handy.

Shelved

Library success isn't just a milestone. It's an asset, one you can point to, draw from, and build on. Don't let it collect dust.

Shelved

Chapter 17: Other Programs That Support Canadian Creators

Beyond the PLR: What Else Is Out There?

While the Public Lending Right (PLR) program is the best-known library-linked payment program for Canadian authors, it's far from the only way creators can receive support. If you're a writer, illustrator, or visual creator working in Canada, you may be eligible for provincial grants, artist development programs, or usage-based royalties even if your books don't qualify for PLR.

This chapter covers the most widely available options, organized by region and funding type. Whether you're applying for a new project, seeking professional development, or looking for additional income from previously published work, it's worth exploring these opportunities.

Provincial Grant Programs for Authors and Illustrators

Most provinces and territories offer project-based or career development funding for literary creators. In many cases, self-published authors and illustrators can apply, especially if the work demonstrates professional merit or community relevance.

Many of these programs are geared toward writers of fiction, nonfiction, children's books, and poetry, but some also support translators, storytellers, spoken word performers, and creators working in hybrid or digital formats.

Below is a list of currently available programs. Be sure to review each funder's eligibility guidelines and deadlines directly on their website, as they change frequently:

Alberta

Alberta Foundation for the Arts (AFA)

AFA offers project grants for individual literary artists, including self-published writers and illustrators in some cases.

British Columbia

BC Arts Council

BC Arts Council offers project and career development grants, including some support for published writers.

Manitoba

Manitoba Arts Council (MAC)

MAC offers grants to writers and illustrators at various stages of their careers, including Indigenous 360 programs and Artists in Schools opportunities.

New Brunswick

ArtsNB

ArtsNB offers creation and career development grants for writers and artists, including those in the literary arts.

Newfoundland and Labrador

ArtsNL

ArtsNL offers professional project grants and travel funding to writers and artists. Literary eligibility includes prose, poetry, and children's literature.

Nova Scotia

Arts Nova Scotia

Arts Nova Scotia has Creation Grants available to writers and literary artists, including self-published creators if work meets professional criteria.

Northwest Territories

NWT Arts

NWT Arts offers project-based funding for individual artists, including literary creators.

Nunavut

Department of Culture and Heritage

The Department of Culture and Heritage provides funding for arts projects, cultural development, and heritage preservation. Writers, storytellers, and artists can apply through programs administered by the territorial government.

Ontario

Ontario Arts Council (OAC)

OAC funds individual creators through project grants and literary programs.

Prince Edward Island

PEI Arts Grants

PEI Arts Grants offers project-based funding for artists, including writers.

Québec

Conseil des arts et des lettres du Québec (CALQ)

CALQ provides project-based funding to Quebec-based literary creators, with streams for French-language and Indigenous work. Some programs have eligibility for self-published work.

Saskatchewan

SK Arts

SK Arts supports authors through literary arts project grants and has specific programs for Indigenous and emerging creators.

Yukon

Yukon Government Arts Fund

Yukon Government Arts Fund offers Advanced Artist Awards, including support for published authors or literary artists working on new material.

Most of these programs include project grants (for writing or illustrating a new work), presentation or travel funding, and sometimes operating support for small presses or independent projects. Some offer special streams for Indigenous creators, newcomers, or emerging artists.

Shelved

Access Copyright – Payback Program

In addition to grant funding, you may also be eligible for royalty payments through the Access Copyright Payback program. This is a separate system from PLR that compensates creators when their work is photocopied or digitally accessed in Canadian institutions such as schools, universities, and government offices.

The Payback program is open to Canadian authors, illustrators, translators, and photographers who have published written or visual content in eligible formats. You don't need to be traditionally published, but your work must have been publicly available in Canada. https://www.accesscopyright.ca/

You'll need to register with Access Copyright and submit a title claim form, listing your qualifying works. Payments are issued annually and may vary depending on your publication history and the usage estimates gathered by the organization.

While the income from this program is usually modest (a few hundred dollars annually for most creators), it can add up over time, especially if you have multiple works or regularly contribute to anthologies, textbooks, or educational materials.

Shelved

Tracking Your Eligibility and Deadlines

Because grant programs and royalties operate independently, it's a good idea to keep a simple tracking system even if it's just a page in your planner or a tab in your spreadsheet that includes:

- Application deadlines (some are once a year, others quarterly)
- Program URLs and contact info
- Eligibility notes (e.g. "must reside in BC," "for published work only")
- Notes on past applications or received funding

Many creators apply for PLR and forget about the rest. But these additional programs, especially at the provincial level, can be powerful tools for expanding your practice, covering project costs, or simply sustaining your career as a creator in Canada.

Using Your Library Footprint to Support Grants

If you're applying for literary funding through the Canada Council, the Ontario Arts Council, or other provincial bodies, don't overlook your library presence as part of your track record. Many applications ask for evidence of public engagement, professional reach, or distribution. You can include a simple line like:

"*My books are held in over 25 public library systems across Canada.*"

Or even more specifically:

"*This title is currently shelved in Toronto, Vancouver, Halifax, and several rural systems in Ontario and Alberta.*"

This kind of placement demonstrates credibility, reach, and lasting value, especially for independently published books. You don't need to frame it as sales; library holdings *are* a form of recognition and access, and granting agencies know that.

Remember the more professionally visible your book is, including library holdings, the more persuasive your applications will be.

Shelved

What Happens Next

If you've made it this far, you already know more about Canadian library systems and the PLR program than most authors ever will. That alone puts you ahead. Whether your book is already in libraries or this is your first step in figuring it out, you're building something sustainable, a way for your work to reach more readers and potentially pay you for years to come.

It's easy to get overwhelmed. There are forms, deadlines, unfamiliar acronyms, and (let's be honest) not a lot of clear guidance for indie authors in Canada. That's why this book exists. You don't need to tackle everything at once. Start small. Get your ISBNs in order and register your title with Library and Archives Canada. Send out your first email to a librarian. Each of these steps opens a door.

If you're reading this before your book is published, keep going. The groundwork you're laying now will make the release smoother. And if your book is already out in the world, it's not too late. You can still submit for legal deposit, pitch to libraries, register for the PLR and start tracking what works for you.

Shelved

This isn't a fast path. But it is a real one.

If you want to stay connected or revisit any of these steps down the line, I'll be adding more on our dedicated page for *Shelved*, as things evolve.

Thanks for trusting me to walk you through it. See you in the stacks!

Jacqueline Cooper

Appendix A: Key Library & PLR Sites

These links will help you take the next steps toward getting your book into Canadian libraries and getting paid if it qualifies for the Public Lending Right (PLR) program.

Library and Archives Canada (LAC)

ISBN Canada

Apply for and manage your Canadian ISBNs.
https://www.collectionscanada.gc.ca/isbn-canada/app/index.php

Legal Deposit Program

Submit a copy of your book to meet the mandatory legal deposit requirement once you have published your work.

https://www.bac-lac.gc.ca/eng/services/Pages/publishers-legal-deposit.aspx

Voilà Catalogue (Union Catalogue)

Search the Canadian national union catalogue, linked with WorldCat.

https://canada.on.worldcat.org/discovery

Shelved

Library Directory (SIGLA)

Search for library systems and contacts across Canada. https://sigles-symbols.bac-lac.gc.ca/eng/Search

Public Lending Right (PLR) Program

PLR Registration Portal

Create an account, make changes and register eligible titles. https://publiclendingright.ca/registration-process

PLR Program Website

Read full eligibility rules, payment thresholds, and FAQs. https://publiclendingright.ca/

Appendix B: Provincial Opportunities for Creators

In addition to national programs like the Public Lending Right, many provinces and territories in Canada offer their own support for authors, illustrators, and other creators. These may include project grants, travel funding, artist residencies, or support for book promotion and marketing.

Each program has its own eligibility criteria and deadlines, and many are only available to residents of that province or territory. If you live in Canada, it's worth exploring what's available locally.

Below is a list of opportunities organized by province and territory. Be sure to verify deadlines and application details directly on each program's official website.

Alberta – Alberta Foundation for the Arts (AFA)
https://www.affta.ab.ca/

Shelved

British Columbia – BC Arts Council

https://www.bcartscouncil.ca/

Manitoba – Manitoba Arts Council (MAC)

https://artscouncil.mb.ca/

New Brunswick – ArtsNB

https://artsnb.ca/

Newfoundland and Labrador – ArtsNL

https://www.artsnl.ca/

Nova Scotia – Arts Nova Scotia

https://artsns.ca/

Northwest Territories – NWT Arts

https://www.nwtarts.com/

Nunavut – Department of Culture and Heritage

https://www.gov.nu.ca/en/culture-language-heritage-and-art

Ontario – Ontario Arts Council (OAC)

https://www.arts.on.ca/

Prince Edward Island – PEI Arts Grants

https://www.princeedwardisland.ca/en/service/pei-arts-grants-funding

Québec – Conseil des arts et des lettres du Québec (CALQ)

https://www.calq.gouv.qc.ca/

Saskatchewan – SK Arts

https://sk-arts.ca/

Yukon – Yukon Government Arts Fund

https://yukon.ca/en/arts-funding

Appendix C: PLR Program Rules Summary

Here's a simplified checklist to help you confirm whether you and your book qualify for Canada's Public Lending Right program:

- You must be a Canadian citizen or permanent resident with a valid SIN number
- You can register up to 20 new titles per year
- You must register each edition separately (hardcover, softcover, eBook, audiobook)
- Books are retired after 25 years or after 5 years of not being found in eligible libraries
- When your last eligible book is retired, your entire file is closed
- You must register through the PLR portal
- Payments are issued once a year in February (minimum $50/year to be paid)
- T4 slips often are not issued unless you receive $500 or more
- You must have a SIN and online banking set up for payment

Shelved

- It is your responsibility to reapply each year for eligible titles
- Payments are taxable income and must be reported

Appendix D: From PCIP to MARC – Example Template

If you've already created a PCIP block for your book, that data can serve as the foundation for a MARC record (Machine-Readable Cataloging). While official MARC records used by libraries follow a strict tagging format, indie authors can create an "unofficial" MARC-style metadata sheet for their own records or to support librarians manually cataloguing their book.

Here's how your PCIP might look:

Sample PCIP Block (Printed on copyright page):

Cooper, Jacqueline

Bye-Bye, Boobies / Jacqueline Cooper.

ISBN 978-1-0694647-01-2 (hardcover)

1. Weaning—Juvenile fiction. 2. Breastfeeding—Juvenile fiction. I. Title.

HQ759.48 .C66 2025

649'.33—dc23

Shelved

MARC-Style Breakdown of the Same Data:

=100 1\$aCooper, Jacqueline

=245 10$aBye-Bye, Boobies /$cJacqueline Cooper.

=264 \1$a[City] :$bLittle Goodbyes Press,$c2025.

=300 \\$a[32] pages :$billustrations ;$c22 cm

=336 \\$atext$btxt$2rdacontent

=337 \\$aunmediatedbn2rdamedia

=338 \\$avolumebnc2rdacarrier

=490 1\$aLittle Goodbyes series

=520 \\$aA gentle picture book about weaning from breastfeeding, narrated by a young child with humor and tenderness.

=650 \0$aWeaning$vJuvenile literature.

=650 \0$aBreastfeeding$vJuvenile literature.

=700 1\$a[Illustrator Name],$eillustrator.

=776 08$iOnline version:$tBye-Bye, Boobies$w(OCoLC)XXXXXXX

=020 \\$a97810694647012

=040 \\$aCaCPLR$beng$erda$cCaCPLR

Creating a MARC Record?

Good news! You don't need to create a full MARC record unless a librarian specifically requests it. And, thankfully, there are also some great tools like MarcEdit https://marcedit.reeset.net/ or library cataloging software that can format this for you.

For most indie authors, simply offering structured metadata (like the above) on your website or in a downloadable file can make your book easier to catalog manually.

Appendix E: Library-Ready Checklist

Quick Checklist: Is Your Book Ready for Library Outreach?

Before you pitch your book to public libraries, make sure you can check off everything below. This list is designed for self-published authors distributing through platforms like IngramSpark, but the same principles apply across the board.

Book Format & Metadata

- ☐ ISBN is registered under your name or imprint (not a free platform-assigned one)
- ☐ Legal deposit submitted to Library and Archives Canada (or your country's equivalent)
- ☐ PCIP block created or alternative MARC metadata available
- ☐ Trim size and spine meet professional print standards (min. 80 pages for spine printing)
- ☐ Front and back covers look bookstore- and library-shelf ready
- ☐ BISAC and subject categories chosen appropriately

Distribution & Listings

- ☐ Listed with IngramSpark, D2D, or other library-accessible distributor
- ☐ Returnable status enabled (at least for Canadian library pitching)
- ☐ Wholesale pricing allows for 30–55% discount to library vendors
- ☐ Metadata (title, author, description, price) is live and correct across platforms
- ☐ WorldCat/Voilà listings checked or expected once legal deposit is processed

Outreach-Ready Materials

- ☐ Short, compelling library pitch email drafted (with local relevance, subject matter hook)
- ☐ Book description tailored to librarians (not just retail buyers)
- ☐ Author or illustrator bio includes community connection or subject expertise

- ☐ You know which libraries you're contacting first (start local, then scale)
- ☐ You're prepared to donate or offer a copy at a discount if asked

Want more links, updates, or bonus tools?

Visit the companion page for this book:

https://www.littlegoodbyes.ca/books/shelved

Glossary

Backlist
A publisher's older titles that are still available for sale, as opposed to new or upcoming releases (called the "frontlist"). Backlist books often generate steady, long-term income.

BISAC codes
Standardized subject categories used in publishing metadata to help retailers and libraries classify your book.

Book returnability
A setting in your distribution setup that allows libraries or retailers to return unsold copies. Often required for library purchasing.

Distributor
A company or platform (like IngramSpark) that makes your book available to retailers, libraries, and wholesalers.

IngramSpark
A print-on-demand and distribution platform commonly used by self-published authors to distribute books to stores and libraries.

ISBN
International Standard Book Number these are a unique identifier assigned to each edition and format of a book.

KDP
Kindle Direct Publishing is Amazon's self-publishing platform for both eBooks and print books.

LAC Legal deposit
A requirement in Canada for publishers and authors to submit a copy of every ISBN-assigned publication to Library and Archives Canada.

Library wholesaler
A company that supplies books to libraries (e.g. Whitehots, Brodart, B&T). Most libraries order through these channels rather than directly from authors.

Little Free Library
A community book-sharing box where anyone can take or leave a book. Often used as a grassroots way to share books locally.

MARC record

A standardized cataloging record format used by libraries to manage and track books in their collections.

Metadata
The set of descriptive details attached to your book that includes title, author, ISBN, BISAC category, and pricing. All used by retailers and libraries to list and classify your title.

PCIP (Preassigned Cataloguing in Publication)
Catalog data formatted for use on a book's copyright page. It helps libraries quickly catalog new titles.

PLR (Public Lending Right)
A Canadian program that compensates creators when their books are found in the holdings of sampled public libraries.

THEMA code
An international book classification system designed to work across global markets. Similar to BISAC codes but more detailed and multilingual-friendly. Used more often outside North America, particularly in Europe.

Trim size
The final physical dimensions of a book after it has been

printed and cut (e.g., 5.5" × 8.5").

This glossary is provided to clarify some of the publishing and library-related terms used throughout the book.

About the Authors

Jacqueline Cooper is a Canadian author, illustrator, and IBCLC. She writes and illustrates picture books for families navigating gentle weaning, early transitions, and childhood milestones through her imprint, Little Goodbyes Press. She is also developing a fairy tale series and other visual projects rooted in storytelling and emotional connection. *Shelved* was created to support fellow Canadian creators looking to get their books into libraries and access programs like PLR. You can find more at www.littlegoodbyes.ca.

Lauren Hoste is a Canadian writer and contributing editor. She supported the development of *Shelved* through editorial input and structural guidance, and collaborates with Jacqueline on future children's book projects. Her work brings clarity, warmth, and reader-focused refinement to each title.

Shelved

Thanks for reading!

If *Shelved* sparked any ideas or offered something useful, consider leaving a quick review or rating wherever you picked it up, it only takes a minute and makes a big difference.

Want to help more authors and illustrators find their way? Share it with your local library or indie bookstore. The more it circulates, the more creators get access to the same tools and support.

Thanks for helping grow the next wave of Canadian creators You're officially part of it now.

www.ingramcontent.com/pod-product-compliance
Lightning Source LLC
Chambersburg PA
CBHW020341010526
44119CB00048B/549